Developing Agro Enterprises Among Farm Women

A Case of Amul

V.M. Rao

2018
Regency Publications
A Division of
Astral International Pvt. Ltd.
New Delhi - 110 002

First Published, 2000
Reprinted, 2018

ISBN: 978-81-87498-14-8 (Hardbound)

Publisher's note:

Every possible effort has been made to ensure that the information contained in this book is accurate at the time of going to press, and the publisher and author cannot accept responsibility for any errors or omissions, however caused. No responsibility for loss or damage occasioned to any person acting, or refraining from action, as a result of the material in this publication can be accepted by the editor, the publisher or the author. The Publisher is not associated with any product or vendor mentioned in the book. The contents of this work are intended to further general scientific research, understanding and discussion only. Readers should consult with a specialist where appropriate.

Every effort has been made to trace the owners of copyright material used in this book, if any. The author and the publisher will be grateful for any omission brought to their notice for acknowledgement in the future editions of the book.

Published by : **Regency Publications**
A Division of
Astral International Pvt. Ltd.
– ISO 9001:2015 Certified Company –
4736/23, Ansari Road, Darya Ganj
New Delhi-110 002
Ph. 011-43549197, 23278134
E-mail: info@astralint.com
Website: www.astralint.com

Acknowledgements

The research report is an outcome of a project sponsored by the Department of Personnel and Training, Ministry of Personnel, Public Grievances and Pensions, Government of India. We are grateful to the Ministry for the support and also for giving permission to publish it in the form of a book.

We are also thankful to Shri B.D. Sharma, Director of the Institute for providing valuable suggestions and also necessary administrative support for conducting the study.

We have received full support and cooperation from the management of Amul in conducting the study. We are specially thankful to Shri Kailas Vyas, Managing Director, the Kaira District Cooperative Milk Producers' union limited for the keen interest evinced and the suggestions provided at various stages of this study. We are thankful to Shri M.K. Sinha (Assistant General Manager), and Dr. A.D. Mujumdar, Deputy Manager (CD of Amul for their valuable suggestions on the report. We are grateful to Dr. S.N. Patel, Deputy Manager (Societies) for arranging trips to villages and also providing access to records of Amul.

During the process of data collection we received help from Shri P.R. Chauhan, Shri S.D. Patel, Shri V.D. Valand, and Shri C.I. Patel (Dairy Supervisors of Amul) and we place on record our thanks to them. Mrs. Jyotsnaben, Mrs. Chandrikaben Shri S.G. Parmar, Shri Rambhai Patel, Shri Maghabhai Parmar, and Shri Kalidas Sewak provided the help in data collection in their respective villages, and also gave insights on the functioning of the society and village dynamics. We are thankful to them. Thanks are also due to the sample respondents who cheerfully spared their time and parted with information sought from them. Their concern for this work which they believed is for improvement of their economic condition is to be appreciated. Special thanks to all women members who gave their free and frank opinion about some of the sensitive questions posed to them.

Thanks are due to Dr. S.N. Singh, General Manager (Cooperative Services) NDDB for sparing valuable time and giving us useful and stimulating feedback and criticism on various points, and Dr. A.A. Chothani, Managing Director (NCDFI) for taking lot of interest on the project. We are also thankful to the management of NDDB particularly Shri H. Ganguli, Advisor, Shri R.K. Makrandi, Manager, and Shri S.K. Ray, Executive, all from the Department of Public Relations, for making necessary arrangements at NDDB.

Sincere thanks are also due to Sh. B.M. Vyas, Managing Director, Gujarat State Cooperative Milk Marketing Federation (GCMMF) for his valuable suggestions on project proposal and subsequently on draft report. Suggestions provided by Dr. S.T. Desai, Manager (Cooperative Services), GCMMF are also acknowledged.

We also benefited from discussions with Profs.V. Ballabh, Sara Ahmed, K.R. Reddy, Rajiv Saxena, Ila Patel and Rajagopal (Institute of Rural Management, Anand), and we would like to record our gratitude to them.

In the initial stages of this study, we had very useful discussions with Prof. S.R. Paranjape, Department of Statistics, and Prof. Sharmila Rege, Department of Sociology, University of Pune and we thank them.

We are thankful to Smt. Ela R. Bhatt, Chair-person, Self-Employed Women's Association (SEWA), Ahmedabad, Prof. Maithreyi Krishnaraj, SNDT University, Bombay, Prof. Shanti George, The Netherlands. Prof. A.H. Somjee and Prof. Geeta Somjee, Simon Fraser University, Canada and Prof. Malcolm Harper, Cranfield School of Management, United Kingdom for their valuable suggestions and incisive comments on the report.

Last but not the least a very many thanks to Miss. S.R. Sannapuri for typing manuscript and also making necessary corrections in the report. Finally, all observations and conclusions are our own and for any short comings we alone are responsible.

Contents

List of Tables

List of Figures

1

Introduction

1.1 Background

Gender equality is central to economic growth and inquality hampers it. Keeping it in mind, way back our ancestors said that 'where women are honoured there the gods are pleased and where they are not honoured all works become fruitless'. In the words of Swami Vivekananda, 'the best thermometer to measure the progress of a nation is its treatment to its women'. Though in ancient times, women in our country were accorded an equal position with men, over time they lost their position. Thus 'too many women in too many countries speak the same language of silence... only her husband had the cosmic right to speak and be heard',[1] which tells us about the condition of women in general and developing countries in particular. The recent report of the UNDP on Human Development reported that 'women work longer hours than men in nearly every country. Of the total burden of paid and unpaid work, women bear an average of 53% in developing countries and 51% in industrialised ones'. Another finding of the report is that unpaid and underpaid women's work accounts for around US $11 trillion in the world economy, which ties in with the legal, economic and political discrimination women face the world over. Their contribution to family income and economy remained largely invisible and unnoticed.

[1] This is a poem presented by Sengupta, A. of Lady Shri Ram College of New Delhi to Mrs. Hillary Clinton during her visit to India in March, 1995 (*Indian Express*, April 1, 1995).

It stems in part from narrow definitions of work as well as from general neglect of household economy and unorganised sector in all statistics. In most parts of the country, daughters are treated as 'paraya dhan'. The committee on status of women had observed a growing deterioration in the status of women from 1911 in the field of education, health, sex ratio, and above all employment (Department of Social Welfare, 1975). Also the characteristics of poor women are aptly recorded as: 'fewer and poor opportunities to work, greater impact of unemployment, under employment, casual nature of work, greater vulnerability due to lack of skills and education, unsafe mobility, heavy responsibilities, a systematic practice of under-rating women's works, and lack of access to better technologies and productive assets' (NCSEWWIS, 1988).

The constitution of India not only provided for equal rights and privileges for women and men but also making special provisions for women. Central Social Welfare Board was established in 1953 to promote and assist voluntary organisations in the field of women welfare, child development, and welfare of the handicapped. Under the community development programme, Mahila Mandals were promoted and supported since second five year plan. Third and fourth plans accorded a high priority to education of women. Fifth plan supported economic development, employment, and training for women as the principal focus for women's socio-economic development. A separate chapter on 'women and development 'was included in the sixth five year plan document and reported that almost despite all these development measures and the constitutional legal guarantees, women have lagged behind men in almost all sectors' (Planning Commission, 1981). A National Commission for Women was set up during January 1992 to study and review the constitutional and legal safeguards provided to women and monitor their implementation (Planning Commission, 1993).[1]

[1] The commission was reconstituted in July 1995 with Mrs. Mohini Giri as the Chairperson. The other members are: Kailash Pati, Ganga Patia, Manorama Singh, Kokila Vyas, Suraiya Mattu, and Annie Prasad will be the member secretary of the commission (*Financial Express*, July 20, 1995).

1.2 Status of Women in India

India has about 407 million women and 60.6% of them are illiterate. The daily work schedule of a rural woman is arduous. The day for her starts in the early hours and she is the last to sleep at night. Time allocation studies show that in developing economies like ours, rural women work an average of 12–18 hours per day, compared to 8–12 hours in case of men. Women today make up 40% agricultural labour force, and yet they are deprived of ownership of land (a strong patriarchal society indeed!). There is ample evidence to show that of the small, marginal, and landless households, women contribute majority of the labour that goes into animal husbandry activities. Though recent studies revealed that the contribution of women is neither marginal nor insignificant (Saradamoni, 1987), their contribution is hardly recognised and their health, education, mobility, employment, etc. were neglected which in turn brought down their status in the society.

1.3 Problem Statement

Dairy farming is a wide-spread economic activity in India, transcending geographic and economic borders. Animal husbandry in many regions had been dominated by the need for draught animals. However, the broad reach of the dairy cooperatives have increasingly caused a shift to milk production. Women are recently beginning to be viewed as important contributors to livestock production systems. In India, about 75 million households are involved in dairying though only 1.45 million women are in women dairy cooperatives. In dairying women are closely involved in tending/cleaning animals and sheds, cutting fodder, fetching grass, feeding, watering, animal health care, hygiene, removing dung, preparation of dung cakes, reproduction, milking, preparation of milk products, marketing, and representation in the organisation of cooperatives. It is estimated that women are responsible for as much as 85% of India's national dairy husbandry activity (NDDB, 1994a). National Dairy Development Board, (NDDB), which is the implementing agency for replication of Anand model in India, realised the role of women in dairying and has been encouraging to enrol them as members. It has also taken the task of establishing 'all women'[1] dairy cooperatives all over the country.

These dairy cooperatives are being organised on similar lines to that of men managed societies. The organisers of NDDB thought that it would be important to involve the women, who are closely associated with dairying, for the overall development of the dairying, family, and finally national economy. As a result about 300 women managed societies have come up in Gujarat state and of them 10 are located in Kaira district (Table 2.10).

1.4 Need for the Study

Women hold up half the sky. They make up nearly 70% of the world's poor and more than 65% of the illiterate (Zhang, 1995). Despite significant progress during 1975–95, (between the first and fourth world women's conference), equality of opportunity and treatment between women and men in the world of work remains elusive as we enter 21st century. Society stands to be the loser for not fully harnessing all of its human resources towards its sustainable development. The primary reason to undertake this study is that there is a saturation in the membership of men in the milk societies and it can only be increased by mobilizing women. The knowledge about the performance of women managed societies vis-a-vis men managed societies would be useful for managerial decision making especially to the organisers of milk unions, government officials and researchers.

Though there are attempts to study the working of 'all women' dairy cooperative societies (Mitra: 1987, 1990; Rao,

[1] Ford Foundation extended financial assistance to Andhra Pradesh Dairy Development Cooperative Federation limited and Bihar State Cooperative Milk Producer's Federation limited respectively during 1983 and 1987 for the formation of all women dairy cooperative societies [Rao R.J. (1985)], All women milk producers cooperative societies in Chittor district, paper presented at the National seminar on women in dairying, organised by the Andhra Pradesh Dairy Development Cooperative Federation limited at Tirupati during December 20–22, 1985, and personal communication from Choudhury, P.N.R.(1995), General Manager, Bihar State Cooperative Milk Producer's Federation limited).

1995; Somjee and Somjee: 1978; and Sundar: 1981), there has not been any comprehensive study so far to compare the performance of women and men managed societies.[1] The above studies on 'all women' dairy cooperative societies also did not consider various physical, financial, managerial, and gender related issues in detail. In the wake of delicensing of dairy sector, it will be important to know the factors responsible for success and/or failure of these societies as it will provide clues to organisers as how to create and sustain member loyalty so as to get continued supply of milk.

In one of the world summits for social development held during 1980 at Copenhagen, it has been asserted that 'attempts shall have to be made to establish structures, policies, objectives, and measurable goals to ensure greater balance and equity in decision making process at all levels and broaden women's political, economic, social, and cultural opportunities and independence and support the empowerment of women'. All-women dairy societies are one such intervention through which women are expected to get both political and economic empowerment by putting democratic organisations in their hands. Hence, it is necessary to see how far they have been successful in achieving one of their objectives. Thus, there is a need to study the performance of both the categories of societies and the impact of all-women societies on the status of women.

1.5 Objectives

The overall objective of the study is to evaluate the performance of women managed dairy cooperatives vis-a-vis men managed dairy cooperatives and draw lessons for future policy planning exercises. The specific objectives of the study are:

(a) to observe the progress of Amul during 1947–95,
(b) to study the socio-economic profile of selected villages and farmers,

---

[1] The study initiated by the Economic Development Associates, on behalf of NDDB, to compare the all women's and mixed gender dairy cooperative societies in selected districts of Andhra Pradesh, Bihar, and Karnataka is yet to be completed.

(c) to analyse the structure and performance of women and men managed dairy cooperative societies and identify factors responsible for success and/or failure of women managed societies,
(d) to understand the status of women during pre and post enrolment in the dairy society,
(e) to work out training needs of the women cooperators for successful operation of the society, and
(f) to document profiles of selected women dairy farmers.

1.6 Methodology

The study made use of both secondary and primary data. Secondary data on the performance of Amul is collected from the records of Amul. Extensive discussions are also held with a number of officials both at Amul and GCMMF to get familiarity with activities of the union.

Multi-stage stratified random sampling technique is adopted in the selection of villages and respondents. Kaira district of Gujarat is purposely selected because of its close association with dairy development in India. Cambay, Anand, and Balasinor talukas are randomly selected to represent three different agroclimatic zones of the district. Thasra taluka is included purposely to study first all-women society in India. On the basis of 'year' of establishment, membership, milk collection, caste composition and distance from the central dairy, 6 villages were selected (3 women managed (all-women) and 3 men managed (mixed gender)). Location of Gujarat in Indian union, location of Kaira district in Gujarat, and location of selected villages in the district are respectively given in Figures 1.1, 1.2, and 1.3. Data on selected villages, and societies are collected from the records of village panchayats and dairy societies respectively. Information on selected parameters of dairy societies are collected for the period 1989–94. Apart from secondary data, information is also collected from 25 respondents selected from each village. Sample farmers are drawn on the basis of size of groups of operational holdings such as landless, small (ha 0.1–2.0), medium (ha 2.1–4.0), and large (ha 4.1 and above). Necessary care is taken to include respondents from all communities and with varying

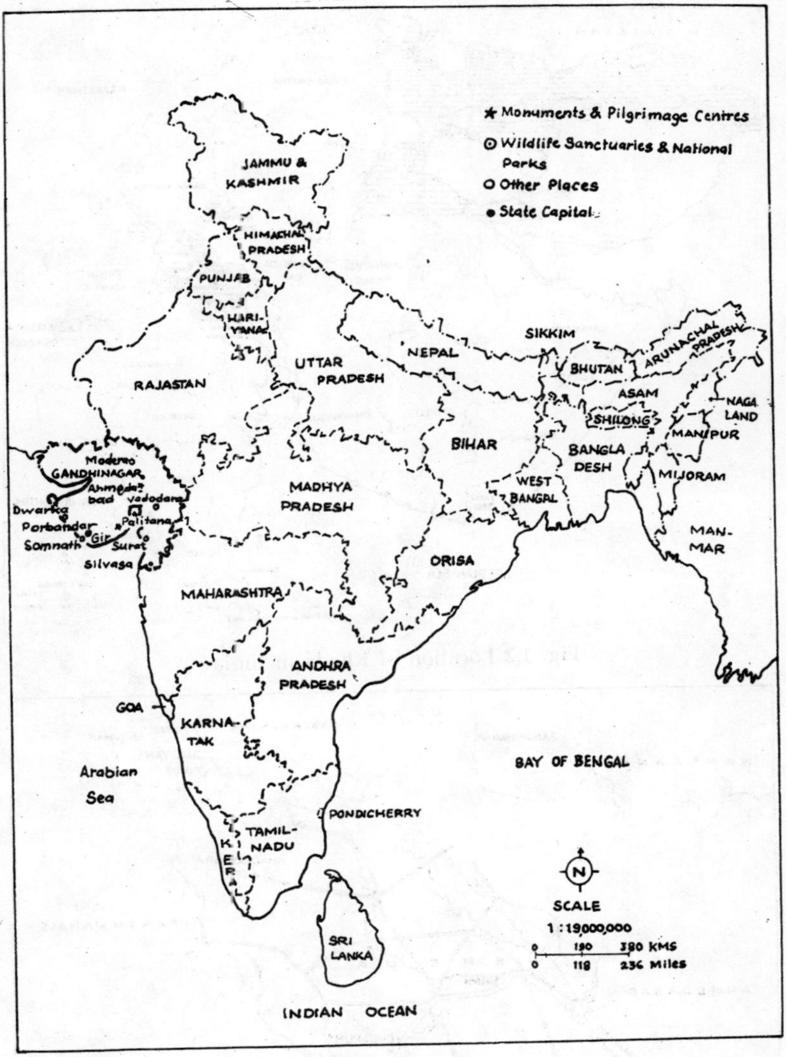

Fig. 1.1 Location of Gujarat in India

animal holdings. The survey is conducted with the help of pretested schedule during February–April, 1995. Separate schedules are prepared for village, society and for respondents.

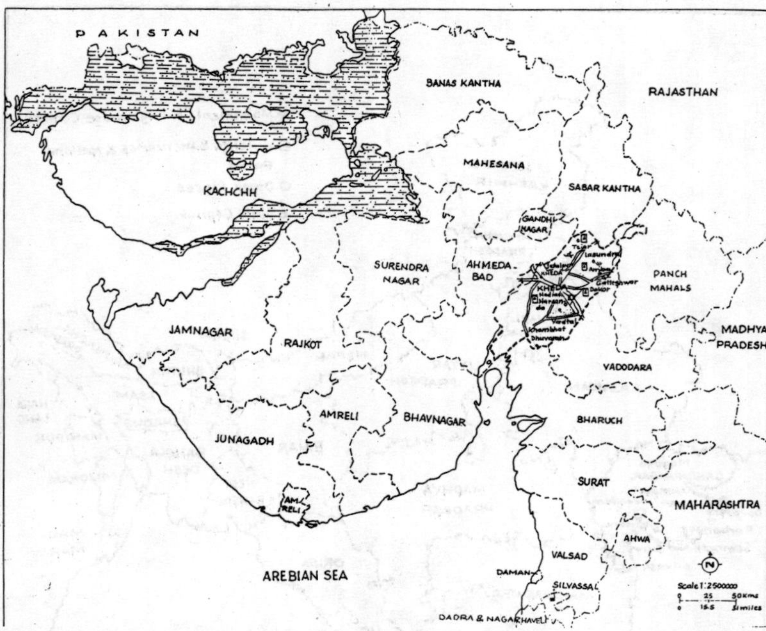

Fig. 1.2 Location of Kheda in India

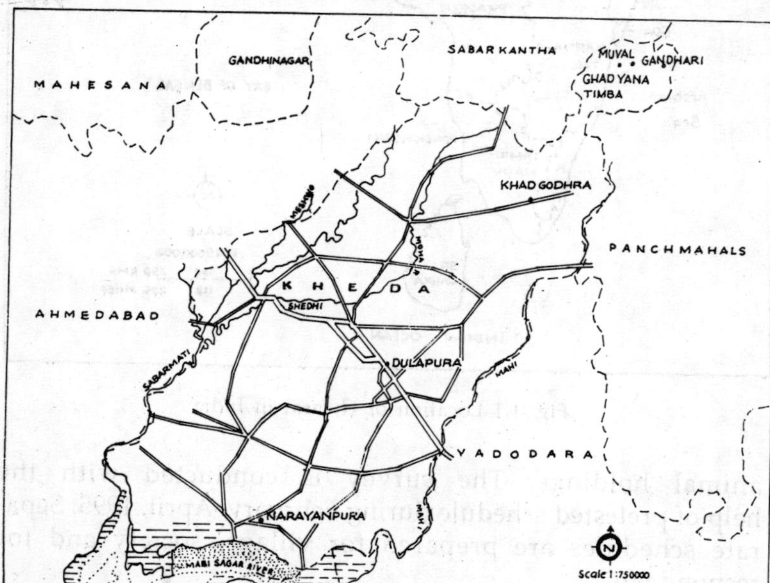

Fig. 1.3 Location of Selected Villages in Kheda

1.7 Organisation of Report

The report is presented in eight chapters. Status of women in dairying, objectives of the study and methodolgoy is presented in Chapter 1. In Chapter 2 Profile of the district and progress of Amul is discussed. Socio-economics of the sample villages and respondents are presented in Chapter 3, and Chapter 4 include the structure and performance of selected dairy cooperative societies. In Chapter 5, status of women during pre and post enrolment in the society are explored and in Chapter 6 effectiveness of cooperative education is examined. Profiles of selected women dairy farmers are provided in Chapter 7 and finally Chapter 8 includes summary and conclusions for policy.

2

Profile of the District and Amul

An attempt is made in this chapter to provide a historical perspective of the district with respect to agriculture and animal husbandry. It is followed by a succinct review of progress made by Amul since its inception.

2.1 District Profile

Kheda district lies in central Gujarat and is banked on the southern side by river Mahi and on north western side by river Sabarmati. The entire district is plain and unbroken except for a small hilly area in northern part of Kapadvanj and Balasinor sub-divisions (talukas) and along the reaches of Mahi where the river bank is cut by deep waters. The district acquires its name from the town of Kheda, the district headquarters and the english people later called it as Kaira. The district has the famous Ranchodrai temple at Dakor and Swaminarayan temple at Vadtal. For the people of Gujarat, Kheda is synonymous with 'charotar', the pleasant land of the Patidar caste (for more details on changing land relations and growth of dairy industry in Kheda, please see Patel, 1990). It is the state's fifth smallest district, measuring 7194 kms and accounting for 3.67% of the state's total geographical area. The district is oblong in shape and one of the most advanced districts of Gujarat as far as agriculture and animal husbandry activities are concerned. The district receives a normal rainfall of 832.1 mm.

2.1.1 Population

The district has a population of 34.41 lakhs of which 16.46 lakhs are women (1991 census). Thus, the district has 3.67% of the total area of the state but, supporting 8.35% of state's population. As against 936 females per 1000 male population at the state level, Kheda has 919 only (Directorate of Economics and Statistics, 1992). According to the latest census, 69.3% of males and 43% of females are literate. There are about 11.59 lakhs main workers in the district (Table 2.1). Of the total main workers, female accounted for only 17.59%. Distribution of cultivators shows male based patriarchal society in which a meagre 5.91% are women cultivators. However, in terms of agricultural labour, women accounted for 30.77% of the total agricultural labour.

2.1.2 Agriculture

According to 1980–81 agricultural census, the district has 3.01 lakh holdings with an area of ha 5.15 lakh. Of the total land holdings, holdings below one hectare accounted for as much as 47.34% in number and only 13.46% in total area (Revenue

Table 2.1: Distribution of main workers of Kheda district, 1991

Category	Number (lakhs)
1. Main workers	11.59
(a) Male	9.55
(b) Female	2.04
2. Cultivators	4.09
(a) Male	3.85
(b) Female	0.24
3. Agricultural labour	3.41
(a) Male	2.36
(b) Female	1.05
4. Household industry workers	0.24
(a) Male	0.19
(b) Female	0.05
5. Other workers	3.85
(a) Male	3.15
(b) Female	0.70

Source : Director of census population (1992), Census of India, 1991, Gujarat series 7, Supplement of paper I of 1991, Government of Gujarat, Ahmedabad.

Department, 1983). In contrast to this, holdings above ha 10 accounted for 0.98% in number and 8.35% in the total area. The district has an irrigated area of ha 3.12 lakhs, and ha 3.15 lakh are unirrigated with ha 27400 of pasture lands and ha 12800 under fodder crops (Directorate of animal husbandry, 1990). As of sources of irrigation, 51.13% is through wells, 34.83% through government canals, and the rest through 'other' sources (tubewells and tanks).

2.1.3 Bovine population

According to 1988 livestock census, it has a total population of 6.48 lakhs of which 5.14% are crossbreds (Table 2.2). Thus, the district has 24% of the total crossbred cows of the state, and 14% of the total state's buffalo population (Directorate of Economics and Statistics, 1991). The district has 344586 milch buffaloes and 77690 milch cows.

2.2 Emergence of Amul

A report written for the Bombay government stated that a Swedish firm has exhibited a cream separator in Nadiad (Kaira district) in 1890. The cream that was separated were sent to Bombay and its separated milk was sent to Ahmedabad and

Table 2.2: Bovine population in Kheda district, 1988

Category	Number	Percentage
Crossbreds		
Male	5006	0.77
Female	33327	5.14
Total	38333	5.91
Local cattle		
Male	155479	23.99
Female	77690	11.99
Total	233169	35.97
Total cattle	271502	41.88
Buffaloes		
Male	32138	4.96
Female	344586	53.16
Total	376724	58.12
Grand Total	648226	100.00

Baroda. Anand taluka took a lead in the manufacture of casein and there were 38 creameries by 1919. During second world war, Polson dairy (a private dairy located in Anand) met a large demand from the defence services. On behalf of the government, it also commissioned and operated a cheese factory in Anand and supplied it to defence services.

In the mid 1940s the colonial government of India contacted Polson to purchase milk from Kaira and supply pasteurized chilled milk to Bombay. As the procurement price was not remunerative, a group of farmers sought the help of Sardar Vallabh Bhai Patel who advised them to boycott the state-supported link with Bombay and to establish their own cooperative societies. On the advise of Shri Patel, Shri Morarji Desai held a meeting at Samarkha (near Anand) on January 4, 1946. It was resolved (a) to organise milk producers' cooperative societies to collect milk from the produces of Kaira district, (b) all such village cooperatives would federate into a district union which would own milk processing facilities, (c) the government should buy milk from the union, and (d) if this was not done, farmers would refuse to sell milk to traders in Kaira district. The government turned down the demand. Farmers called milk strike which lasted 15 days. Milk commissioner of Bombay visited Anand and accepted farmers' demand. This marked the beginning of the Kaira District cooperative Milk Producers Union Limited, which was formally registered on December 14, 1946.

2.2.1 *Management of Amul*

The union is controlled by board of directors consisting of 21 members of which 12 are democratically elected from amongst the representatives of the primary societies, 3 representatives from the Government of Gujarat, and one each from individual members, Kaira District Central Cooperative Bank, Gujarat Cooperative Milk Marketing Federation (GCMMF) , National Dairy Development Board, Cooperative Department of Government of Gujarat. Managing director is the member secretary. Shri Tribhuvandas Kishibhai Patel was its founder chairman during 1946–73 and 1978–79. Organisational chart of Amul is presented in Appendix A.

It has two chilling centres (Balasinor and Kapadvanj), Amul Research and Development Association (ARDA), chocolate and malted milk foods factory (Mogar), and cattle feed plant (Kanjari). Construction of a modern 650 thousand Kg milk per day capacity Amul-3 is in progress. Foundation stone for a modern cheese plant at Khatraj (Mehmadabad) was laid in 1994 and efforts are on to have a chilling centre at Cambay. Thus, in all about 2300 employees are working in various units of the union.

2.2.2 *Progress of Amul*[1]

The progress of the union is presented in Table 2.3. There were thirteen milk societies with a membership of 924 and the value of sale of the union was Rs. 0.79 million during 1948–49. There is a gradual increase in the number of societies, and it went up to 610 and the total membership was 1.75 lakhs with the value of sale of the union being Rs. 271.93 million by 1969–70. The union introduced five AI centres during the 1950–51. The number has increased to 475 by 1969–70 and 1.52 lakh inseminations were carried out during that year. The progress continued, and by 1993–94, there were 943 milk cooperative societies with a membership of 5.13 lakhs and total milk collected was 277 thousand tonnes. Of the total milk collected, cow milk contributed to as much as 34%. The value of the sale of the union was Rs. 3289 million. Further, the union sold about 145 thousand tonnes of cattle feed to member societies. One can infer from the above facts that there is substantial growth in all the parameters considered in Table 2.3. This growth is mostly contributed to the forward and backward linkages provided by the union, members loyalty, dedicated employees, and above all committed leadership.

While the above facts spoke of the performance of Amul since its inception, they do not provide relative performance of Amul with other 12 milk union affiliated to GCMMF. Hence, an attempt is also made to provide an overview of cooperative dairying in Gujarat.

---

[1] Progress of Amul in terms of production of fluid milk, butter cheese, ghee, casein, chocolates, nutramul, powder, etc. are not considered here (for details on these aspects see Patel, 1995).

There are 12 milk unions under GCMMF with 8926 societies (Appendix B). In all there are 16.81 lakh members in the state of Gujarat of which 30.52% are covered by the Kaira milk union. Similarly, there are 2.92 lakhs women members in the state of which 32.54% are covered by Mehsana union and 25.69% by Kaira union. Total annual milk procurement of the GCMMF was 10.89 lakh tonnes and the contribution of Mehsana and Kaira is about 51.51%. The average annual milk collected per member is the highest in Mehsana (1005 litres) followed by the Banaskantha, Sabarkantha, Surat, Ahmedabad, Valsad, and Kaira. The average annual milk collection per member in Kaira milk union is 527 litres only.

2.2.3 *Growth in share capital and reserve fund*

The growth of the union in terms of the paid up share capital and the reserve fund are shown in Table 2.4. The paid up share capital was Rs. 0.41 lakhs during 1947–48 and it went up to Rs. 34.72 lakhs by 1970–71 and further increased to Rs. 205.57 lakhs by 1993–94. Similarly, reserve fund of the union has also increased from Rs. 6.94 lakhs in 1955–56 to Rs. 363.20 lakhs in 1993–94. Thus, both paid up share capital and reserve fund of the union has increased substantially during the study period.

2.2.4 *Price of kg fat*

Members loyalty can be earned by providing services like cattle feed, fodder seeds, fodder saplings, technical advise, artificial insemination facilities, health care facilities and remunerative price to the produce. Of all the facilities, price of the milk/litre paid to the producer plays a major role in procuring more and more milk from the members. For this reason average price of kg fat paid by Amul during the period 1949–95 is presented in Table 2.5. The price of kg fat was just Rs. 7.45 during 1948–49 and went up to Rs. 15.27 by 1970–71 and further increased to Rs. 77.03 by 1989–90. Since then there is an appreciable increase in the price paid by the union. The rate of kg fat paid by the union is Rs. 140 during 1994–95 and this is considered to be one of the highest in the country.

Table 2.3: Progress of Kaira District Cooperative Milk Producers' Union Limited (Amul), 1949–95

Financial year	Milk coop. societies	Membership	Milk collection (000 tonnes)	Milk collection centres (owned by societies)	AI centres	AIs performed	Mobile veterinary dispensaries	Cases treated by mobile dispensaries	Sale of cattle feed (000 tonnes)	Value of sale (Rs. millions)
1948–49	13	924	1.14	—	—	—	—	—	—	0.79
1949–50	27	1995	2.73	—	—	—	—	—	—	1.72
1950–51	33	3973	5.00	—	5	578	—	—	—	3.40
1951–52	53	8882	9.09	—	11	786	2	—	—	6.12
1952–53	62	11307	12.41	—	7	1314	2	—	—	8.26
1953–54	64	14441	10.86	—	6	1673	2	—	—	6.80
1954–55	64	18983	11.73	—	6	2574	2	—	—	8.15
1955–56	64	22828	11.14	—	7	3854	2	—	—	7.49
1956–57	107	26795	14.17	—	14	5533	2	7796	—	8.95
1957–58	130	29003	21.16	—	14	6434	2	6435	—	13.41
1958–59	138	33068	27.56	—	14	6287	2	6958	—	21.17
1959–60	167	40181	22.93	—	14	7700	3	6986	—	18.22
1960–61	195	40500	23.92	—	26	9077	4	16453	—	19.85
1961–62	219	46400	35.40	—	44	12839	4	18811	—	31.52
1962–63	254	58500	50.42	—	75	19232	5	24669	—	45.62
1963–64	378	65000	62.30	—	102	26148	5	33520	—	60.36
1964–65	421	85000	60.64	—	138	31582	6	29886	4.19	62.73
1965–66	518	110000	65.91	—	261	41841	7	31777	15.91	92.22
1966–67	567	120000	71.61	—	312	87445	12	46583	24.11	117.64
1967–68	592	135000	80.60	—	332	104306	12	54829	24.45	148.88
1968–69	600	148000	113.16	—	362	137808	15	60548	31.20	241.91

1969–70	610	175000	123.88	160	475	151985	16	62842	42.87	271.93
1970–71	706	180000	118.23	210	523	157547	16	70078	36.86	273.94
1971–72	744	215000	133.22	266	550	156823	19	74254	41.97	336.04
1972–73	783	225000	147.81	320	581	157316	21	89931	51.31	392.24
1973–74	794	235000	111.95	348	571	150419	21	79886	50.73	316.18
1974–75	844	245000	130.95	372	668	192626	21	96659	59.87	446.46
1975–76	829	250000	129.04	412	665	207674	23	118258	46.27	427.26
1976–77	831	255000	127.02	445	678	222000	23	121310	63.95	442.00
1977–78	831	275000	141.20	460	711	248263	21	159219	70.85	535.53
1978–79	856	295000	159.26	495	734	255011	21	135041	77.78	581.13
1979–80	895	308000	169.38	509	739	268792	22	136081	82.54	664.24
1980–81	895	327000	169.58	521	735	285073	23	133695	82.33	753.00
1981–82	894	339000	160.02	527	731	325886	23	145199	99.35	785.67
1982–83	895	352000	183.82	537	704	353152	18	124198	98.06	953.61
1983–84	880	359000	182.02	558	722	354744	18	123043	110.82	1030.48
1984–85	870	359000	193.22	584	736	422876	18	143080	131.74	1224.80
1985–86	872	365000	227.26	606	759	497174	18	183614	152.65	1334.19
1986–87	877	407000	213.77	628	779	514004	18	115840	154.45	1525.01
1987–88	890	423000	212.93	650	779	563270	18	59625	157.71	1614.59
1988–89	900	436000	204.73	667	788	627057	18	58607	136.44	1790.19
1989–90	904	457000	263.10	694	809	678288	16	64810	113.88	2145.00
1990–91	917	474850	264.83	711	809	681497	16	67364	132.90	2504.60
1991–92	923	487400	233.89	728	811	690385	16	54615	140.46	2690.60
1992–93	941	502550	260.18	731	819	696713	16	55894	145.78	3114.70
1993–94	943	513280	277.36	739	826	721073	16	60030	144.51	3289.00
1994–95	954	532670	229.21	751	827	672852	16	41003	144.16	3445.00

Source: Records of Amul

Table 2.4: Growth in share capital and reserve fund of Amul, 1948–95

Year	Paidup share capital (Rs. in lakhs)	Reserve fund (Rs. in lakhs)
1947–48	0.41	NA
1950–51	0.72	NA
1955–56	3.17	6.94
1960–61	7.41	14.82
1965–66	13.71	70.45
1970–71	34.72	168.93
1975 -76	52.93	220.92
1980–81	89.62	243.12
1985–86	156.53	277.78
1986–87	171.30	285.82
1987–88	186.49	296.60
1988–89	205.11	308.38
1989–90	205.44	320.83
1990–91	204.75	332.31
1991–92	204.75	342.73
1992–93	204.58	352.99
1993–94	205.57	363.20
1994–95	235.43	373.19

NA = not available
Source: Records of Amul

2.2.5 Mode of milk collection and complaints

The union has 113 milk routes through which it collects milk from all the 943 societies. Thus, milk is being collected twice in a day directly to the union's plant at Anand and 2 chilling centres located in different directions of the district. The union paid Rs. 21.48 lakhs per month towards transport charges during 1993–94. The longest distance is 60 kms and the milk comes from the societies between 8.00–11.30 am while evening milk collection at Anand is between 7.30–10.30 pm. Of the 113 routes, 45 are run with the help of milk societies own vehicles. The average transportation cost/litre of milk worked out to be Rs. 0.10 during 1993–94 while it was Rs. 0.07 during 1989–90.

When the milk is received by the union there are instances of discrepancies in the quality and quantity of milk. Further, complaints are also noticed in case of cattle feed. There were as many as 9143 complaints in 1969–70 and they increased to 36267 by 1993–94 (Table 2.6). These complaints can be catego-

Table 2.5: Average price of kg fat at Amul, 1949–95

Year	Rs./kg fat
1948–49	7.45
1949–50	7.39
1950–51	7.33
1951–52	7.30
1952–53	7.11
1953–54	7.10
1954–55	6.60
1955–56	6.41
1956–57	6.50
1957–58	6.50
1958–59	6.69
1959–60	7.43
1960–61	7.61
1961–62	7.90
1962–63	7.92
1963–64	8.14
1964–65	8.50
1965–66	9.50
1966–67	11.35
1967–68	13.11
1968–69	14.81
1969–70	14.90
1970–71	15.27
1971–72	15.73
1972–73	15.76
1973–74	19.70
1974–75	27.01
1975–76	24.36
1976–77	24.19
1977–78	26.46
1978–79	27.80
1979–80	28.96
1980–81	30.00
1981–82	35.54
1982–83	39.73
1983–84	41.92
1984–85	49.58
1985–86	51.52
1986–87	55.45
1987–88	65.60
1988–89	77.20
1989–90	77.03
1990–91	80.59
1991–92	102.04
1992–93	109.59
1993–94	104.20
1994–95	124.52

Source: Records of Amul

Table 2.6: Complaints registered with Amul, 1970–95

Year	No. of Complaints
1969–70	9143
1970–71	8080
1971–72	7401
1972–73	8071
1973–74	9473
1974–75	12186
1975–76	14651
1976–77	13911
1977–78	17709
1978–79	17878
1979–80	20778
1980–81	22991
1981–82	19718
1982–83	20352
1983–84	24426
1984–85	22036
1985–86	20402
1986–87	22102
1987–88	21882
1988–89	25761
1989–90	25290
1990–91	27762
1991–92	35103
1992–93	37586
1993–94	36267
1994–95	33302

Source: Records of Amul

rised into (a) shortage of milk, (b) shortage in weight of cattle feed, (c) poor quality cattle feed, (d) shortage in fat percent, and (e) any other. These complaints are brought to the notice of the union which are attended by the milk procurement officer for investigation. As a part of this exercise, society's registers are verified, details for the month are calculated, and the adjustments are made accordingly. After establishing the truth the milk procurement officer calls members of the society and explains about action taken. Such unbiased, and prompt actions taken on the complaints inspired the members and enhanced their loyalty to the union. During the year 1990–91, 27762 complaints were received wherein 4.26 lakh litres of milk was involved and as against this, complaints involving 2.40 lakh litres were settled. Similarly, in the year 1993–94 complaints for a quantity of 6.11 lakh litres of milk were received of which 3.08 lakh litres were settled. Thus, the amount for which the complaints are rejected is negligible and comes to little less than a litre (874ml) per society/day. Of the total milk received in 1993–94, 0.94% was sour and 1.92% was grade II milk.

2.2.6 Village chilling units

Village chilling units have been provided in 12 villages of the district to enable farmers procure and supply clean, chilled, and fresh milk (1993–94). As a result of this, Amul milk collection trucks do not have to visit such societies twice a day, since the milk produced by its members is safely stored against attack from bacteria. It has relieved milk producers of the binding to supply milk within the time frame of arrival and departure of trucks. The village societies can now fix collection time suitable to milk producers. The approximate cost of the unit with a capacity of 2000 litres is about Rs. 5.00 lakhs.

2.2.7 Electronic milk collection stations

Electronic units to calculate fat, weight, and price thereof each time milk is poured as also cumulative for 10 days have been installed at societies who opted for. This on-line electronic equipment ensures its members access to complete transactions in no more than five minutes. Batches of milk samples no longer have to be taken to testing room since the new milk testers instantly measure the fat content of the milk immediately after it is weighed. Based on this test, an electronic billing machine produces an account of how much is owed to each producer for his/her milk. Approximate cost of this machine is Rs. 1.00 lakh and Rajasthan Electronics and Instruments Limited, Jaipur is the manufacturer.

2.2.8 Cooperative development programme

This programme is being organised in the villages by the union and the district cooperative union with the assistance of GCMMF, and National Dairy Development Board.

2.3 Women in Dairying

Milch animals are mainly tended by women in India. For families with dairy animals, a significant proportion of women's energy and time is spent on household level milk production. It is estimated that women are responsible for as much as 85% of India's national dairy husbandry activity. On an average, a woman with a dairy animal spends more than 2.5 hours in its feeding, watering, cleaning, and milking (NDDB, 1994). Hence, the beneficial impact of any dairy husbandry programme should depend upon the extent to which women feel its importance and significance. Further, modern rural women are quite conscious of their contribution towards family income, they always remain eager to raise their income from sale of milk through services provided by the milk union. Amul believed that through cooperative dairying rural women can acquire formal recognition for themselves and can also show their managerial skills as principal managers of their own business enterprises. Their capacity and potential in organising cooperatives, managing their business, democratic decision making, and maintenance of records were also realized (ESCAP, 1981).

2.3.1 Growth in women membership

The percentage of women to total membership was just 7.6% during 1960–61 and it increased to 13.12% by 1989–90 which further increased to 14.6% by 1993–94. Thus, there is a gradual increase in the coverage of women by the milk co-operative union. As a result of it, there is a decline in the percentage of male members to the total membership (Table 2.7). With a view to bring awareness and make them part of the union's activities, Amul has been trying to bring women members to visit Amul and informing them about its activities. Such an exercise made a positive impact and women members started realising that Amul has been working for their benefit. The number of women visiting Amul increased from 1415 in 1961–62 to 26725 by 1993–94 (Table 2.8).

Table 2.7: Growth of women membership at Amul, 1961–95

Year	No. of societies	Members		
		Male	Female	Total
1960-61	195	37,422	3,078	40,500
1970-71	706	1,63,620	16,380	1,80,000
1977-78	831	2,56,427	18,573	2,75,000
1980-81	895	2,94,300	32,700	3,27,000
1981-82	894	3,00,000	39,000	3,39,000
1982-83	895	3,07,000	45,000	3,52,000
1983-84	880	3,14,300	44,700	3,59,000
1984-85	870	3,14,300	44,700	3,59,000
1985-86	872	3,23,000	42,000	3,65,000
1986-87	877	3,58,000	49,000	4,07,000
1987-88	887	3,71,000	52,000	4,23,000
1988-89	900	3,81,500	54,500	4,36,000
1989-90	904	3,97,200	60,000	4,57,200
1990-91	917	4,11,000	63,850	4,74,850
1991-92	923	4,21,100	66,300	4,87,400
1992-93	941	4,30,660	71,890	5,02,550
1993-94	943	4,38,330	74,930	5,13,280
1994-95	954	4,53,970	78,700	5,32,670

Source: Records of Amul

2.3.2 *Women mahila seminars*

Since 1968, management of Amul has been giving importance to the formation of 'all-women' dairy co-operative societies. The basic idea was to bring women into decision making process by involving them in the management of business enterprises. In order to bring awareness among women members, the union has started organising mahila seminars from December 1980 and it is being continued till date. It is a 3 day programme and lady instructors identified the potential villages and women and conduct programmes from 12 noon to 4 pm in their villages. The programme covers cooperative dairying, linkages of primary society with the union, cooperative philosophy, role of women in dairying, animal nutrition, etc.

On the third day, women participants are taken to Anand to have an exposure to the on-going developmental activities at the union's level. There is no payment for attending this programme but some snacks are provided during the period. In the initial year (1980–81) 20 milk societies were covered

Table 2.8: Growth in ladies visits to Amul dairy, 1962–95

Year	No. of societies covered	No. of ladies visited Amul
1961–62	6	1415
1962–63	2	600
1963–64	45	11805
1964–65	32	6972
1965–66	25	4800
1966–67	74	19807
1967–68	47	9746
1968–69	64	12236
1969–70	40	8845
1970–71	50	8565
1971–72	22	4914
1972–73	51	10565
1973–74	16	2276
1974–75	25	3849
1975–76	43	7840
1976–77	35	5955
1977–78	31	5700
1978–79	37	5960
1979–80	31	5710
1980–81	40	7282
1981–82	90	16002
1982–83	98	16311
1983–84	82	13247
1984–85	72	14641
1985–86	77	15597
1986–87	83	16071
1987–88	32	6454
1988–89	85	17539
1989–90	108	27960
1990–91	27	6550
1991–92	27	7810
1992–93	34	8135
1993–94	113	26725
1994–95	97	14860

Source: Records of Amul

and about 2000 women trained under this programme. The number of societies covered increased to 317 by 1993–94 and about 28000 women were trained (Table 2.9).

2.3.3 'All-women' societies

As mentioned earlier, women have been playing an important but invisible role in dairy husbandry sector. They had

Table 2.9: Mahila seminars organised by Amul, 1981–95

Year	No. of societies covered	No. of mahilas trained
1980–81	20	2035
1981–82	143	17288
1982–83	191	25296
1983–84	159	20782
1984–85	142	22063
1985–86	190	26071
1986–87	172	17902
1987–88	164	16810
1988–89	208	19833
1989–90	158	12457
1990–91	173	11708
1991–92	112	8325
1992–93	296	22906
1993–94	317	27938
1994–95	341	31485

Source: Records of Amul

very little role in decision making either to purchase an animal or to sell, or to keep the money earned out of this enterprise. Though they worked hard, they are dependent on menfolk for their daily requirements. Attempts have been made to provide access to money and power by various agencies. The task was also carried out by Kaira milk union way back in 1968.

The first 'all-women' dairy cooperative society in India was established at Khadgodhra, Thasra taluka of Kaira district in 1968. Some of the researchers described it as a managerial shift and lauded it as a successful case (Somjee and Somjee: 1978, 1989; and Sundar: 1981). However, for various reasons now known to us promotion of 'all-women' societies was not pursued by 'Amul' and as on today there are only ten such societies in the district. The details of 'all-women' managed societies are provided in Table 2.10 of which four societies are yet to complete one full year. Further, Taraghaiya society was closed because of inadequate milk procurement.

2.4 Taluka-wise Status of Dairy Cooperatives

As mentioned in the initial paragraphs the union has covered all the 10 talukas of the district and taluka-wise details are

Table 2.10: Details of 'all-women' managed societies at Amul, 1993–94

Name	Taluka	Members	Annual milk No. of (litres)	No. of employees
Khadgodhra	Thasra	366	2,22,619	4
Muval	Balasinor	81	1,54,157	3
Ghadiyana Timba	Balasinor	78	1,87,704	3
Sultanpagina suvada	Balasinor	166	1,98,013	3
Gorpuralat	Balasinor	117	71,667	2
Taraghaiya	Thasra	84	22,675	12*
Nandanvan	Petlad	150	NA	3
Valinath	Thasra	171	NA	2
Lolpura	Borsad	253	NA	2
Piparia	Matar	240	NA	3

*Closed due to inadequate milk procurement.
Source: Records of Amul

provided in Table 2.11. Kapadvanj taluka has the highest number of milk societies followed by Nadiad, Anand, and Balasinor. Out of the 943 milk societies, 78% of them have their own buildings. As regards quantum of milk collected, as many as 12% of them are having a collection of less than one lakh litres/year, 52% of them with a collection ranging between 1–3 lakh litres per year, 22% of them with a collection of 3–5 lakhs, and the rest, 14%, have collection of more than 5 lakhs per year. As of average milk procurement, Petlad taluka stood first followed by Borsad, Cambay and Anand. Percentage of sour milk to the total milk collection was the lowest in Petlad taluka and the highest in Thasra taluka. This is primarily because of their location and distance from the processing/chilling centre. Anand taluka is nearer to the Amul factory whereas Thasra taluka is some 60–70 kms away from the milk union.

2.5 Summary

Kaira district has the advantage of good soil, improved buffaloes, hard working, sincere and innovative farmers, entrepreneurs like Pestonji Polson, committed leaders like Sardar Vallabh Bhai Patel, Morarji Desai and Tribhuvandas Patel, and technocrats like Dr. V. Kurian and his colleagues. Amul

Table 2.11: Taluka-wise details of milk societies at Amul, 1993–94

Particulars	Anand	Balasinor	Borsad	Cambay	Kapadvanj	Mehmedabad	Matar	Nadiad	Petlad	Thasra	Total
1. No. of societies	102	98	92	76	165	76	68	103	87	76	943
2. Own buildings	90	51	90	58	110	56	61	85	81	57	739
3. Milk collection (less than 1 lakh kgs.)	6	12	3	3	34	9	7	14	6	18	112
1-3 lakh kgs.	54	64	46	41	86	40	33	53	18	54	489
3-5 lakh kgs.	25	13	23	12	27	23	21	21	38	3	206
More than 5 lakh kgs.	17	7	22	20	18	6	7	15	23	1	136
4. Total milk procured ('000 tonnes)	33.61	21.76	35.14	28.61	40.37	22.40	20.19	28.82	34.94	12.49	278.32
5. Average milk procured (tonnes)	330	227	382	376	245	295	297	280	411	164	296
6. % of sour milk	0.32	0.72	0.83	1.18	1.02	2.04	1.62	0.82	0.14	2.09	0.95

Source: Records of Amul

was evolved out of the felt needs of farmers, supported by the local leaders and has a huge urban market for the milk produced in rural areas. Though there was some government protection in the initial period, combined efforts of farmers, leaders and technicians lead the milk union to come out as one of the few successful examples in India. There is a spectacular growth in almost all the performance parameters studied during the period 1947–95. Interestingly, the management of Amul realised the role of women in dairy farming, and did considerable work to bring them under the fold of cooperatives.

3

Socio-economics of Selected Villages

An attempt is made in this chapter to provide an overview of selected villages followed by a brief description of the selected milk societies.

3.1 Salient Features of Selected Villages

As mentioned earlier there are 10 talukas in Kaira district and selected villages are drawn from 4 talukas representing 3 different ecologies. From among the selected talukas, three each with men and women managed societies are identified for the purpose of detailed analysis. As of women managed societies, there are only 5 societies who have completed more than five years of which four are located in Balasinor taluka and one in Thasra taluka (Table 2.10). Hence, two societies from Balasinor and one from Thasra are included in the study. Gandhari, a mixed gender society, is as far as 140 kms away from Anand while Dalapura, again a mixed gender society, is as close as 8 kms from Anand (Table 3.1). Narayanpura (mixed gender) and Khadgodhra (women managed) societies are 65 kms each away from the Amul factory. Dalapura has the highest population (1560) and Ghadiana Timba has the lowest (125). Of the 6 societies, Patels' are economically and politically prominent in as many as 4 villages. Kshatriyas are dominant in rest of the 2 villages. Thus, these 2 castes are dominating in the management of the dairy societies in the selected villages. As of total agricultural land it is the highest in Khadgodhra. However, it is to be mentioned here that

Table 3.1: Salient features of the selected villages

Particulars	Muval	Ghadiana Timba	Khadgodhra	Narayanpura	Dalapura	Gandhari
Taluka	Balasinor	Balasinor	Thasra	Cambay	Anand	Balasinor
Distance from Anand (km)	125	115	65	65	08	140
Total population	225	125	1481	500	1560	996
Major Castes	(a) Patel (b) Kshatriya	(a) Patel (b) Carpenter	(a) Kshatriya (b) Patel (c) Muslim (d) Vankar (e) Barber	(a) Patel (b) Kshatriya (c) Potter	(a) Kshatriy (b) Bariya	(a) Patel (b) Brahmin (c) Vankar (d) Blacksmith (e) Kshatriya
Total agricultural land (acre)	175	237	1750	355	265	1039
Source of irrigation	(a) Tubewell (b) Well (c) Rain	(a) Canal (b) Well (c) Rain	(a) Well (b) Rain	(a) Tubewell (b) Well (c) Rain	(a) Canal (b) Well (c) Rain	(a) Tubewell (b) Well (c) Rain
Crops grown Kharif	Maize,Rice Bajra, Gram Sesamum	Rice, Maize Bajra, Gram	Rice, Bajra Tobacco, Gram Sesamum, Bajra	Rice	Bajra	Maize, Cotton Rice, Gram
Rabi	Mustard, Wheat Sunflower, Lucerne	Wheat, Oliyali	Bajra, Wheat Rapeseed, Groundnut	Tobacco, Jowar Mustard, Wheat Lucerne	Wheat, Lucerne	Wheat, Rapeseed, Sunflower
Summer	Bajra, Groundnut Chikori	Bajra, Groundnet Lucerne	Bajra	Bajra, Lucerne	Bajra, Maize	Bajra, Lucerne
Area under green fodder (acres)	52	30	29	92	18	120

Source: Records of selected villages.

Khadgodhra is considered to be the poorest in the district with regard to its natural resource base. Most of the land is rocky and dry and agriculture is completely dependent on rains. Only small pieces of land are irrigated by the 9 wells which can be used for 2–3 hours a day. The name of the village is believed to be operational from the words 'Khed' and 'Godhra' which means it is a land where only grass and fodder can be grown (ESCAP, 1981).

In all the 3 men managed societies there is an adequate ground water availability and the total land is fairly on the higher side compared to women managed societies. As of source of irrigation only a small portion of the total land is irrigated under canal water in Dalapura and Ghadiana Timba, while in the rest of the villages the major sources are well, tubewell and rain. From the point of view of crops a number of cash crops and oil seeds are grown on these lands in all the 3 seasons. There are wide variations in the area under green fodder in the 6 selected societies. It is as high as 30% to the total agricultural land in Muval and as low as 1.66% in Khadgodhra and the rest are in between.

3.1.1 *Infrastructural facilities*

Infrastructure is another important variable which contributes to be success or otherwise of any firm/industry. Infrastructure in terms of electricity, metal roads, post office, telephone, school, PACS, etc. are presented in Table 3.2. A close perusal of Table 3.2 reveals that the villages are not well endowed with the facilities considered. Though, there are variations across sample villages, the villagers are to walk between 1.5 km and 10km to get these facilities. All the women managed societies have locational disadvantages which is reflected through non availability of these facilities. It is true with Gandhari also.

3.1.2 *Milch animal population*

Since milch animals are important for successful operation of dairy societies, an attempt is made to provide the details of animals in selected villages. An interesting observation which

Table 3.2: Infrastructure facilities in the selected villages

Facility	Muval	Ghadiana Timba	Khadgo-dhra	Narayan-pura	Dala-pura	Gand-hari
Electricity	Yes	Yes	Yes	Yes	Yes	Yes
Metal road	3.0km	7.0km	Yes	Yes	Yes	Yes
Bus stop	1.5km	Yes	Yes	1.0km	Yes	1.0km
Post office	1.50km	1.0km	Yes	2.0km	2.0km	Yes
Telephone	Yes	Yes	Yes	Yes	Yes	Yes
Library	6.0km	Yes	10.0km	4.0km	2.0km	Yes
High school	6.0km	Yes	10.0km	4.0km	2.0km	1.5km
Bank	6.0km	1.0km	10.0km	4.0km	2.0km	10.0km
Vaterinary hospital	6.0km	2.0km	10.0km	4.0km	2.0km	10.0km
Primary health care centre	6.0km	2.0km	1.5km	4.0km	7.0km	10.0km
Fair price shop	1.5km	2.0km	Yes	4.0km	7.0km	Yes
PACS	6.5km	5.0km	Yes	4.0km	7.0km	10.0km
Public well	No	No	Yes	No	Yes	Yes

Source: Records of selected villages

can be made from Table 3.3 is that local buffaloes are kept only in Khadgodhra village which shows its relative backwardness over other villages. Similarly, the proportion of local cows is marginal to total milch animals in all the selected villages. In absolute number, total milch animals are the highest in Narayanpura followed by Khadgodhra and it is the lowest in Gadhiana Timba. If we compare Tables 3.1 and 3.3, villages having higher population/higher agricultural land have more number of animals than otherwise. Though the number of crossbreds is higher in Narayanpura village the percentage of crossbreds to total stock is higher in Muval and Gadhiana Timba.

The number of animals, both crossbreds and improved buffaloes, are more in Narayanpura because they availed the facilities from the social welfare board of the Government of Gujarat. Under this scheme, 20 women members were given 3 milch animals each at a unit cost of Rs. 15000. Similarly, the village availed the facility of 'Yuvak Sahakari Dairy Pashu Palan Yojana' financed by the Amul Research and Develop-

Table 3.3: Milch animal population in the selected villages

Village	Crossbred cows	Local cows	Improved buffaloes	Local buffaloes	Total
Muval	69	24	97	—	190
Ghadiana Timba	102	5	71	—	178
Khadgodhra	3	26	150	165	344
Narayanpura	190	37	228	—	505
Dalapura	3	1	304	—	308
Gandhari	27	26	195	—	248

Source: Records of selected villages

ment Association (ARDA).[1] Under this scheme, 10 youth were selected and were given 5 crossbred animals with a total outlay of Rs. 50000 per youth. While selecting the beneficiaries care was taken to select (a) unemployed and those who are interested in the profession, and (b) those who have land. The scheme was financed by the state agriculture and rural development bank and started in December, 1994

3.2 Key Indicators of Selected Societies

The details of selected dairy societies are provided in Table 3.4. Dalapura and Khadgodhra and to some extent Gandhari are the societies established prior to 1970 and the rest 3 started functioning from the later half of 1980s.

Though, there is no representation of men members in women managed societies, membership is open to all persons in men managed societies. There are 5 employees in Narayanpura society and 4 each in Dalapura, Gandhari and Khadgodhra, while Muval, and Gadhiana Timba have 3 employees each.

Though Khadgodhara is an 'all women' society, the employees are men. During its 27 years of existence, it has not been successful in finding out suitable women employees to

---

[1] ARDA was formed by Amul and is engaged in conducting research on infertility in cattle, nutritional problems, fat and SNF problems in milk, etc. The ARDA also provide some financial help through district central cooperative bank. Women benefit from the results achieved by ARDA when the information is passed on to them through various media such as mobile exhibitions, film shows, and TV programmes.

Table 3.4: Key indicators of dairy societies in the selected villages, 1995

Indicator	Muval	Ghadiana Timba	Khadgo-dhra	Narayan-pura	Dala-pura	Gand-hari
Date of registration	15-6-1988	23-12-1988	2-10-1968	10-10-1986	14-3-1966	18-6-1970
Manage-ment	Female	Female	Female	Male	Male	Male
Member-ship	Male 00 Female 83 Total 83	Male 00 Female 53 Total 53	Male 00 Female 396 Total 396	Male 201 Female 85 Total 286	Male 211 Female 52 Total 263	Male 214 Female 9 Total 223
Number of Mgt. committee members	09	09	09	09	09	09
Building	Rented	Rented	Owned	Panchayat blg.	Owned	Owned
Number of employees	03	03	04	05	04	04
Sex of the employees	Female	Female	Male	Male	Male	Male
Society assets (Rs.)	25, 577	35,028	48,734	38,625	1,64,462	77,834

Source: Records of selected societies

manage the society. It is to be mentioned here that this is the first 'all-women' dairy society in India and Shrimati Jasumatiben Mehta was instrumental in forming the society. She was a widow, hails from brahmin community (a minority community in the village) and assertive. She was a dynamic and selfless woman dedicated to upliftment of villagers. She succeeded in mobilizing the village women to form their own milk cooperative in 1968 and continued as chairperson till July 1976. Subsequently, things went wrong and there were problems with administration, thefts, communal disputes, etc.[1] The union intervened and now things are better. Societies with longer life recorded higher fixed assets compared to societies of recent origin.

[1] In our opinion, it was organised by Amul as show piece. Jasumatiben failed in appointing women as employees in the society and could not develop second tier leadership. Further, after her tenure men started taking revenge on women and they went to the extent of beating women for attending adult education classes. Finally, it became a male chauvinistic society.

3.2.1 Physical and financial performance

Physical and financial performance of the selected milk societies for the year 1993–94 are given in Table 3.5. Total milk collection is highest, 2.31 lakh litres, in Narayanpura and lowest, 1.36 lakh litres, in Dalapura. Cost of milk procurement per litre of milk collected is the lowest in the Ghadiana Timba followed by Muval.

About 3% of milk procured in Gandhari society became sour while it is 0.15% in Khadgodhra. Thus, except Gandhari, spoilage in other societies is on the lower side. Necessary precautions may be taken to reduce this quantity as it acts adversely on the incomes. Cattle feed sold per litre of milk procured is the highest in Narayanpura and the lowest in Gandhari. In terms of training programmes conducted, Narayanpura society did well compared to other societies studied. As many as 115 persons are trained in Narayanpura while it is the lowest (4 persons) in Gandhari. As there was no substantial increase in milk procurement, Ghadiana Timba and Khadgodhra obtained audit class B while others have A category. All the committee members in men managed societies are literate while it ranged from 55–78% in women managed societies. A comparison of women *vs* men managed societies from the same taluka (Balasinor) also indicated the superiority of women over men.

3.3 Socio-economics of Selected Farmers

Apart from studying selected milk societies, a moderate sample of 25 members are also interviewed to understand social, and economic conditions of the dairy farmers. Proper care has been taken to select members from different communities and also with different land and animal holdings. What follows are the details of selected dairy farmers. On an average above 29% of members in men managed societies are less than 35 years of age and another 44% are between 36 and 50 years (Table 3.6). As against this about 12% of women are less than 25 years of age and as many as 48% of them are between 26 and 35 years and thus 60% of women members are less than 35 years of age.

Table 3.5: Comparison of selected milk societies, 1993–1994

Particulars	Muval	Ghadiana Timba	Khadgo-dhra	Narayan-pura	Dala-pura	Gand-hari
Milk collection (lakh litres)	1.56	1.87	2.16	2.31	1.36	1.62
Cost of milk collection (Rs./litre)	0.35	0.29	0.49	0.44	0.45	0.39
Sour milk (litres)	487	818	317	1029	38	6167
Cattle feed sold (bags of 70 kg)	489	850	1557	1549	750	430
Cattle feed sold /litre of milk procured (kgs)	0.220	0.318	0.504	0.478	0.378	0.186
Training programmes conducted	4	3	3	11	2	1
People trained	81	40	120	150	37	4
Audit class	A	B	B	A	A	A
Literate committee members (%)	55.6	77.8	66.7	100.0	100.0	100.0

Source: Records of selected villages

As of literacy, about 37% of women members are illiterate as against 21.3% in men (Table 3.7). Interestingly, percentage of members studied between 6–10th standard are higher in women managed societies, while men out numbered women in other two categories.

3.3.1 *Land-wise and animal-wise distribution*

The details on land-wise distribution of sample dairy farmers are given in Table 3.8. It is to be mentioned here that only 6 of the 75 women households have land on their name. Rest of them have reported the land owned by their husbands. It is customary in the Indian society that the land and other fixed assets are owned by men[1]. However, women work on lands most of the time than men and their work is invisible. Table 3.8 shows that about 58.7% of the women members have land ranging from ha.0.1–2.0 while only 5.3% have land about

[1] The existing land ownership pattern in India is largely male oriented except in some areas of north-east and a few other places where matrilinial system is in operation and inhertence of property passes through the institution of mother [for more details, see NDDB, (undated)].

Table 3.6: Age-wise distribution of sample dairy farmers

Village	Up to 25	26–35	36–50	51 and above	Total
Muval	3 (12.0)	17 (68.0)	4 (16.0)	1 (4.0)	25 (100.0)
Ghadiana Timba	6 (24.0)	15 (60.0)	4 (16.0)	0 (0.0)	25 (100.0)
Khadgodhra	0 (0.0)	4 (16.0)	16 (64.0)	5 (20.0)	25 (100.0)
Sub-total	9 (12.0)	36 (48.0)	24 (32.0)	6 (8.0)	75 (100.0)
Narayanpura	1 (4.0)	10 (40.0)	9 (36.0)	5 (20.0)	25 (100.0)
Dalapura	1 (4.0)	8 (32.0)	10 (40.0)	6 (24.0)	25 (100.0)
Gandhari	0 (0.0)	2 (8.0)	14 (56.0)	9 (36.0)	25 (100.0)
Sub-total	2 (2.6)	20 (26.7)	33 (44.0)	20 (26.7)	75 (100.0)

(Figures in parenthesis indicate percentages to sub-total)
Source: Field study

ha.4.0. As regards men managed societies, the situation is much clear. As many as 83% of the total farmers have land between ha 0.1–2.0. Thus, it can be safely concluded that dairying is owned and managed by small and medium farmers in both women and men managed societies. Of the total 150 households, just 4% of them have land above ha 4.0.

In similar manner, the ownership of milch animals is also analysed and given in Table 3.9. It is customary in the communities of Patel, Kshatriya, Brahmin, and Blacksmith that at the time of marriage women get one or two animals (big or small) from her parents (peer). Thus, these animals are considered as property of the women and the incomes accrued out of these animals are sometimes kept as Stridhan by women. This income is in turn used for children's education, purchase of clothes for children, purchase of household articles, and any other items which women consider necessary. There are instances when this money is also taken over by men. As compared to ownership of land as many as 36% of women interviewed have their own animals given by their parents.

Table 3.7: Literacy levels among sample dairy farmers

Village	Illiterate	Up to 5	6–10	11 and above	Total
Muval	11 (44.0)	4 (16.0)	9 (36.0)	1 (4.0)	25 (100.0)
Ghadiana Timba	2 (8.0)	3 (12.0)	18 (72.0)	2 (8.0)	25 (100.0)
Khadgodhra	15 (60.0)	6 (24.0)	4 (16.0)	0 (0.0)	25 (100.0)
Sub-total	28 (37.4)	13 (17.3)	31 (41.3)	3 (4.0)	75 (100.0)
Narayanpura	4 (16.0)	5 (20.0)	12 (48.0)	4 (16.0)	25 (100.0)
Dalapura	9 (36.0)	6 (24.0)	10 (40.0)	0 (0.0)	25 (100.0)
Gandhari	3 (12.0)	9 (36.0)	8 (32.0)	5 (20.0)	25 (100.0)
Sub-total	16 (21.3)	20 (26.7)	30 (40.0)	9 (12.0)	75 (100.0)

(Figures in parenthesis indicate percentages to sub-total)
Source: Field study

Interestingly, the distribution of milch animals is more equitable than the distribution of land holdings. Members having one animal is around 16% in women managed societies, 21% have two animals, 27% have 3 animals, 22.7% have 4 animals, and 13.3% have more than 5 animals. Interestingly, there are only about 3% of members having 4 animals in men managed societies. The percentage of people having animals upto 3 is 72.

3.3.2 *Production, consumption and disposal of milk*

An attempt is also made to understand the production, consumption, and disposal behaviour of milk among selected dairy farmers, and the data are provided in Table 3.10. Average production of milk per household/year is the highest, 4475 litres, in Ghadiana Timba and the lowest, 1509 litres, in Khadgodhra. Total production per household/year in Muval is 4311 litres while the average annual production in men

Table 3.8: Land-wise distribution of sample dairy farmers

Village	Landless	ha.0.1–2.0	ha.2.1–4.0	ha.4.1 and above	Total
Muval	0 (0.0)	15 (60.0)	8 (32.0)	2 (8.0)	25 (100.0)
Ghadiana Timba	0 (0.0)	15 (60.0)	8 (32.0)	2 (8.0)	25 (100.0)
Khadgodhra	6 (24.0)	14 (60.0)	5 (20.0)	0 (0.0)	25 (100.0)
Sub-total	6 (8.0)	44 (58.7)	21 (28.0)	4 (5.3)	75 (100.0)
Narayanpura	2 (8.0)	22 (88.0)	1 (4.0)	0 (0.0)	25 (100.0)
Dalapura	7 (28.0)	18 (72.0)	0 (0.0)	0 (0.0)	25 (100.0)
Gandhari	0 (0.0)	22 (88.0)	1 (4.0)	2 (8.0)	25 (100.0)
Sub-total	9 (12.0)	62 (82.6)	2 (2.7)	2 (2.7)	75 (100.0)

(Figures in parenthesis indicate percentages to sub-total)
Source: Field study

managed societies varied between 1370 and 2742 litres. It can be inferred from Tables 3.1, 3.3, and 3.10 that Ghadiana Timba and Muval have less agricultural land, and milch animals but produce more milk per household. In other words, milch animals maintained in these two villages are of high genetic potential. Further, these two villages are well off in terms of quality land, financial position, education, awareness, use of improved techniques, etc. compared to other villages studied. Of the total milk produced as high as 84–85% is sold to milk societies in Muval, and Ghadiana Timba while it is 66–68% in Gandhari and Dalapura. There are absolutely no sales to 'others' (private milk traders, tea shops, sweet makers, neighbourers, etc.) in Narayanpura, Gandhari, Muval, and Ghadiana Timba. Dalapura is close to Anand and there are 3 private milk traders who carry milk to Anand. As of Khadgodhra, members sold some milk to neighbourers who don't have milch animals.

Table 3.9: Ownership of milch animals among sample dairy farmers

Village	1 animal	2 animals	3 animals	4 animals	5 and above	Total
Muval	2 (8.0)	4 (16.0)	9 (36.0)	5 (20.0)	5 (20.0)	25 (100.0)
Ghadiana Timba	2 (8.0)	1 (4.0)	7 (36.0)	10 (40.0)	5 (20.0)	25 (100.0)
Khadgodhra	8 (32.0)	11 (44.0)	4 (16.0)	2 (8.0)	0 (0.0)	25 (100.0)
Sub-total	12 (16.0)	16 (21.3)	20 (26.7)	17 (22.7)	10 (13.3)	75 (100.0)
Narayan-pura	2 (8.0)	11 (44.0)	5 (20.0)	0 (0.0)	7 (28.0)	25 (100.0)
Dalapura	14 (56.0)	9 (36.0)	1 (4.0)	1 (4.0)	0 (0.0)	25 (100.0)
Gandhari	8 (32.0)	10 (40.0)	3 (12.0)	1 (4.0)	3 (12.0)	25 (100.0)
Sub-total	24 (32.0)	30 (40.0)	9 (12.0)	2 (2.7)	10 (13.3)	75 (100.0)

(Figures in parenthesis indicate percentages to sub-total)
Source: Field study

3.4 Utilization of Savings

It can be observed from Table 3.10 that, on an average, 2817 and 1397 litres of milk is sold to societies in women and men managed societies respectively. Thus, the total gross income from the sale of milk would be around Rs. 18677 in women managed societies and Rs. 10003 in men managed societies. Assuming that, 80% of this income would be required to be spent on fodder, feed, labour, health care, insurance, interest on fixed capital, etc. dairy farmers are left with an annual net income of Rs. 3535 in women and Rs. 2001 in men managed societies. Here the value of home grown fodder, family labour, etc. are imputed and included in the total cost of milk production. Further, value of milk consumed at home, value of dung, and value of calf are not considered in calculating the net income from dairying. Utilization pattern of these savings is presented in Table 3.11.

As farmers gave multiple answers hence totals don't add up to 25 in each village. Members in women managed socie-

Table 3.10: Production, consumption, and disposal of milk among selected dairy households

Village	Average production (litres)	Average home consumption (litres)	Sales to society (litres)	Sales to others (litres)
Muval	4310.7 (100.0)	750.4 (17.41)	3560.3 (84.59)	—
Ghadiana Timba	4475.0 (100.0)	714.5 (15.97)	3760.5 (84.03)	—
Khadgodhra	1509.0 (100.0)	354.0 (23.46)	1129.0 (74.82)	26.0 (1.72)
Average	3431.6 (100.0)	606.3 (17.7)	2816.6 (82.1)	8.7 (0.2)
Narayanpura	2742.1 (100.0)	574.6 (20.95)	2167.5 (79.05)	—
Dalapura	1370.4 (100.0)	425.2 (31.03)	934.2 (68.17)	11.0 (0.80)
Gandhari	1660.9 (100.0)	571.0 (34.35)	1089.9 (68.17)	—
Average	1924.5 (100.0)	523.6 (27.2)	1397.2 (72.6)	3.7 (0.2)

Source: Field study

ties utilized their savings mostly on (a) purchase of consumer durables, (b) purchase of milch animals, (c) purchase of gold, (d) ceremonial functions, etc. These savings are also utilized for children's education. Quite interestingly, the proportion of men respondents utilized their savings on purchase of milch animals, whereas purchase of gold and consumer durables is comparatively less as compared to women respondents.

3.5 Summary

Selected villages represented three different ecologies of Kaira district. Of the 6 societies, three were established prior to 1970 and rest in the later half of 1980s. In terms of quality of soil, availability of ground water, productivity of animals, general economic conditions, etc., Khadgodhra is in a disadvantageous position. There is a positive correlation between population/ agricultural land and bovine population but negative correlation between size of the stock and productivity. As a result

Table 3.11: Utilization of savings among sample dairy farmers

Purpose	Muval	Ghadiana Timba	Khadgo-dhra	Narayan-pura	Dala-pura	Gand-hari
Purchase of consumer durables	20	16	18	15	16	10
Cerimonial functions	4	5	15	10	9	9
Purchase of milch animals	15	11	4	6	9	4
Purchase of gold	10	13	8	4	2	2
Children's education	6	3	2	8	5	5
Repayment of old loans	—	—	—	4	—	—
Purchase of land	—	—	5	7	2	1
Purchase of agricultural implements	1	3	1	2	1	1

Note: It is assumed that decisions in the utilization of savings in women managed societies are taken by women only and men in the men managed societies. In certain households it may not be correct. However, results in chapter 5, by and large, supports our assumption.
Source: Field study

cost of milk procurement per litre of milk collected is the lowest, Rs. 0.29, in Ghadiana Timba while it is the highest, Rs. 0.49, in Khadgodhra. Average age of women members is relatively less than men members. The distribution of land holdings is more skewed than the distribution of animal holdings. Similarly, only 8% of women members have land on their name while as many as 36% of them have their own animals. About 82% and 73% of milk produced is sold to the milk societies in women and men managed societies respectively; sales to 'others' are negligible. Women utilized their savings on purchase of consumer durables, milch animals, gold, etc., while men gave priority to consumer durables, ceremonies and milch animals in that order.

4

Structure and Performance of Dairy Societies

An attempt is made in this chapter to study structure and performance of women managed dairy cooperative societies vis-a-vis men managed societies. For this purpose data from 1989–90 to 1993–94 are considered and the averages are presented in the following sections.

4.1 Structure of Dairy Cooperative Societies

A person can become member of the society provided (a) he/she is residing in the area of operation and has completed 18 years of age, (b) he/she has a buffalo/cow for milk production and supplying milk to the society for 3 consecutive months preceding the date of his/her application, and (c) he/she has taken at least one share of Rs. 10 and paid the entrance fee.

All the members of the society those who have supplied milk for not less than 180 days in a year or supplied 700 litres in the previous cooperative year (July–June) are eligible to exercise their vote to elect a 9 member managing committee to the society. These 9 members will elect a chairperson from among them, who is assisted by a vice chairperson (there is no provision for vice chairperson in the byelaws). The day-to-day operations of the society are looked after by the secretary who is assisted by milk tester and milk collector and are employees of the society. The term of the chairperson is one year and one third of the committee members are elected every year (for more details on byelaws, see NDDB, 1987). With a view to decentralise the power, and manage society efficiently, various internal committees have been constituted. They included: (a) purchase committee, (b) members grievances committee, (c) internal auditor, etc. The same procedure is being followed in all the milk societies in Kaira district. These primary societies are in turn affiliated to the Kaira District Cooperative Milk Producers' Union Limited, Anand, which is also known as Amul.

4.2 Performance of the Selected Societies

Performance of commercial organisations is generally measured in terms of financial performance, growth, staff well being, system viability and adaptability, and good corporate citizenship (Steers, 1975). However, organisations working primarily for the welfare of the rural people like dairy cooperatives cannot be evaluated using these criteria alone. They need to be evaluated also on a set of criteria pertaining to their impact on socio-economic conditions of the beneficiaries (Khandwalla, 1987). Thakur (1974) has examined the progress of selected milk cooperatives in Gujarat and concluded that Amul, Dudhsagar, Banas, and Sabar have made remarkable progress. The performance of dairy cooperatives was measured with the help of 25 indicators and found that major strength of the unions in Gujarat, besides providing marketing support to the milk producers, lies in their ability to provide—and importance attached to—regular medicare services for the milch animals (Reddy and Sharma, 1990). According to the authors, coverage of most villages under regular veterinary services not only helped in enabling the maintenance of milch animal's health but also build up a strong phychological bond between the producers and the unions. This in turn helped in developing the loyalty of milk producers to the unions. Shah, 1991 also provided a detailed analysis of a primary dairy cooperative society and analysed the performance with the help of membership, milk collected, its value, gross sales per member, average base price/litre of milk, net profit, etc. In his rapporteur's report on 'learning from success: analytical review of case studies of successful farmers and farmer's cooperative', Shah identified (a) service to members, (b) financial indicators, (c) autonomy and self reliance, (d) impact on member incomes, (e) strategies for viability and growth, and (f) leadership and management as parameters of success (Shah, 1990). Sen and Rani (1990) also analysed the management of women dairy cooperatives in Andhra Pradesh. Based on the above review of literature, an attempt is made here to evaluate the performance of two categories of societies, namely women managed and men managed.

4.2.1 Physical and financial performance

As explained earlier the selected societies are drawn from 4 talukas of the district with varying agro climatic situations. The physical and financial performance of these societies for the period 1990–94 are provided in Table 4.1. Careful observation of Table 4.1 reveals that membership in women

Table 4.1: Physical and financial performance of milk societies, 1990–94

Indicator	1989–90		1993–94		1990–94	
	Women	Men	Women	Men	Women	Men
Membership	161	239	177	257	171	248
Milk collection (lakh litres/ year)	1.59	1.52	1.86	1.76	1.77	1.62
Average milk contribution per member (litres/year)	987	636	1052	685	1035	653
Value of milk (Rs. in lakhs)	6.42	6.91	10.59	11.06	9.21	9.25
Average value of milk poured per member (Rs.)	3989	2890	5982	4305	5386	3731
Average sour milk (litres/year)	—	—	541	2411	*1527	*2343
Net profit (Rs.)	54303	48412	47829	94394	57712	80748
Total expenditure (Rs.)	35109	42945	70419	75455	47785	56974
Cost of procurement (Rs./litre)	0.22	0.28	0.38	0.43	0.27	0.35
Reserve fund (Rs. in lakhs)	0.40	0.54	1.04	1.69	**1.04	**1.69

Note: Of the 3 women managed societies, performance of Khadgodhra is poor in relation to size of population, land and stock of animals. Other two are in between 'moderate' to 'good'. All the 3 man managed societies are of 'moderate' performance. Hence, comparison is made on the basis of their averages.

* Average of 1993–95
** Position as on 30-6-1994
Source: Records of selected societies

managed societies is less by 45% than in men managed societies. This is mainly due to the fact that 2 out of the 3 women managed societies are formed recently after getting delinked from the earlier men managed societies. Moreover, membership in the women managed societies is restricted to women only while all persons having milch animals are eligible to become members in the men managed society (Rao, 1995). Thus, the membership in the men managed societies is on the higher side. However, there is gradual increase in the membership in both categories. Coming to milk collection (lakh litres/year), it is the highest in women managed societies in all the 3 periods studied. During 1990–94, on an average women managed societies collected 1.77 lakh litres/year while men managed societies collected 1.62 lakh litres/year. This difference is more perceptible when we worked out the average milk contribution per member (litres/year) which came to 1035 litres in women managed societies as against 653 litres in men managed societies. Thus, members in women managed societies poured 42% more milk than their counterparts in the men managed societies. This difference can also be seen from value of milk, and the average value of milk poured per member.

Milk is highly perishable and the shelf-life is about 3–4 hours after taking from the udder of the animal. Since, these villages are located away from the main processing plant/chilling centre, it takes some time to reach the chilling centre/processing plant for necessary processing. In case the time taken to reach the processing plant is more, the milk gets spoiled and becomes sour. The milk can also get spoiled when malpractices are followed by the members in the form of adding preservatives, supplying previous days milk, pouring the newly calved animal's milk, pouring the milk of sick animals, etc.

The average sour milk in the selected societies is 541 litres in women managed societies and 2411 litres in men managed societies. In percentage terms, sour milk is 0.29% of the total milk collected in women managed societies and 1.34% in men managed societies. However, there is some improvement and the quantity of sour milk declined in both the categories for the period 1993–95.

Another important factor noticed in the study is the cost of procurement per litre of milk handled. This cost works out to be Rs. 0.22 per litre of milk in women managed societies and Rs. 0.28 per litre in men managed societies (1989–90). More or less similar results are also noticed for the period 1990–94. The low cost of procurement in women managed societies can be attributed to (a) less unnecessary expenditure, (b) minimum leakages, (c) good financial management, and (d) more volume of milk collected. All these factors together contributed to low cost of procurement in women managed societies. The men managed societies have been functioning since long and as expected the reserve fund in these societies are on the higher side. The only exception is Narayanpura society which was established in 1986.

From the above discussion, one can conclude that women managed societies are performing relatively better than men managed societies[1]. However, comparison for a longer period will be more appropriate to arrive at a concrete conclusion in this regard and lack of historical data on women managed societies is one of the drawbacks of the study.

These cooperative societies have been providing a number of services to its members which include (a) milk collection, (b) local sale of milk for the consumers, (c) supply of cattle feed and fodder seeds, (d) artificial insemination facilities, (e) health care facilities, (f) cattle insurance, (g) member insurance, etc. While all these services offered by the cooperatives are valued highly by members, direct economic benefit in terms of price of milk, and the price differences paid by the union and the cooperative are the most important to the members (Shah, 1991).

The distribution of economic returns per litre of milk are provided in Table 4.2. The average base price is Rs. 5.20 per litre of milk in women managed societies while it is Rs. 5.71 in men managed societies. This difference in base price is due to supply of cow milk in the women managed socieites. About 15% and 13% more on base price is received by women and men managed societies respectively in the form of their un-

[1] A comparison of women vs men managed societies also revealed the superiority of women over men (for more details, see chapter 3, Tables 3.3 to 3.5, and 3.10).

Table 4.2: Distribution of returns per litre of milk, 1990-94

(amount in rupees)

Particulars	1989-90		1993-94		1990-94	
	Women	Men	Women	Men	Women	Men
Average base price	4.04	4.55	5.69	6.29	5.20	5.71
Union's price difference	0.41	0.41	0.52	0.52	0.45	0.45
Society's price difference	0.23	0.22	0.35	0.27	0.29	0.25
Membership bonus	0.05	0.05	0.07,	0.08	0.06	0.06
Total returns	4.73	5.23	6.63	7.16	6.00	6.47

Source: Records of selected societies

ion's price difference, society's price difference and membership bonus. There is a possibility to increase this difference by increasing the volume of trade at the society level and also through production of value added products at the union level.

4.2.2 *Bovine holding*

As milch animals are the basic raw materials to transform inputs into milk, details on these animals in the selected societies are collected and presented in Table 4.3. As expected both breedable cows and buffaloes are more in number in men managed societies. In absolute numbers, there are 265 breedable bovines in women managed societies and 354 in men managed societies. However, if one recalls the total milk procurement, it is the highest in the women managed societies. Thus, one can conclude that the animals in the women managed societies are superior to animals maintained in the men managed societies. It is to be mentioned here that all the cows maintained in the women managed societies are crossbreds. Similarly, average bovines held per member is the highest in the women managed societies than in men managed societies. The average area under fodder crops, however, is relatively less in women managed societies. As mentioned earlier these societies have been supplying a number of milk production enhancement inputs to its members. Cattle feed sales per litre milk collected worked out to be 0.410 kg in women managed societies and it is slightly higher (0.430 kg) in men managed societies (Table 4.4). The recommended level of cattle feed per litre of milk produced is 0.500 kg which is almost close to what has been observed in the field study.

Table 4.3: Bovines holding in the selected societies

Particulars	Women	Men
Breedable cows	80	95
Breedable buffaloes	185	259
Total breedable bovines	265	354
Average bovines per member	1.5	1.4
Average area under fodder (acres)	30.67	79.00
Area under fodder/animal (acre)	0.12	0.17

Source: Records of selected societies

Table 4.4: Progress in technical inputs supplied by milk societies, 1990–94

Indicator	1989–90		1993–94		1990–94	
	Women	Men	Women	Men	Women	Men
Cattle feed sales (bags)	924	914	965	944	1026	990
Cattle feed sales (kg/litre)	0.41	0.42	0.36	0.38	0.41	0.43
Artificial inseminations performed	175	245	244	342	201	291
Animals conceived	51	71	78	89	62	85
Rate of conception (%)	29.1	29.0	32.0	26.0	30.8	29.2
First aid cases treated	210	489	130	580	176	552
Cattlesheds constructed	18	15	20	8	19	13

Source: Records of selected societies

Similarly, performance of artificial insemination is better in men managed societies (the number of animals in men managed societies are higher!). However, rate of conception is better in women managed societies probably due to better attention and care given by the women. The conception rate worked out to be 31% in women managed societies and 29% in men managed societies. Women managed societies availed facilities of construction of cattle sheds, with the help of Amul, to a greater extent compared to their counterparts. As the men managed societies are older in age, may be members in these societies have already availed these facilities in the past.

4.3 Qualitative Aspects

Having seen the financial and physical performance of the societies, an attempt is also made to identify some of the qualitative aspects in the management of these societies. Composition of management committee members is one such factor considered and the details are given in Table 4.5. The average age of the committee members is 35.8 years in women managed societies and 46 years in men managed societies. Thus, relatively younger people are exposed to maintain business enterprises among women than among men. In a patriarchal society, mostly it is the age and experience which is given more weightage than creativeness, education, and intelligence. However, women managed to come out of this age old tradition and elected only qualified young and energetic women to run cooperative societies. As regards educational status of these members, about one third of them in women managed societies are illiterate and the rest studied upto 10th standard. However, all the committee members in the men managed societies are literate, about 11% of them have

Table 4.5: Composition of management committee members, 1994–95

Particulars	Women	Men
Total members/society	9	9
Average age of committee members	35.8	46.0
Education status		
(a) Illiterate (%)	33.3	0.0
(b) Upto 5th standard (%)	22.2	44.4
(c) 6–10th standard (%)	44.5	44.4
(d) 11th and above (%)	0.0	11.2
Caste-wise distribution		
(a) Chairperson	Patel - 1 Muslim - 1 Sutar - 1	Brahmin - 1 Patel - 1 Kshatriya - 1
(b) All committee members (%)		
Brahmin	0.0	11.1
Patel	63.0	29.6
Kshatriya	18.5	48.2
Blacksmith	0.0	3.7
Sutar	3.7	0.0
Muslim	7.4	0.0
Vankar	7.4	7.4
Average number of committee meetings held	14.0	13.7
Average attendance	7.6	7.5
Frequency of interaction with officials of Amul	Weekly	Fortnightly

Source: Records of selected societies

studied 11th and above. Thus, one may conclude that the educational status of the women committee members is relatively low compared to their counterparts in men managed societies. Efforts will have to be made to encourage and convince parents to send their daughters to schools. Recently announced government decision to provide mid-day meals in schools may act as an incentive in this regard. Education improves horizons, widen our thinking and makes the person think rationally. The social bias against sending girls to school is still prevalent, stemming from the belief that women's rightful place is within the home. But the children of an educated mother will have a better chance of completing their education than those of an illiterate woman. Besides, an educated woman will have a greater say in the affairs of family and even in the society. It is hoped that such a change certainly will help women to be self reliant and independent.

As regards milk pouring members, little less than 50% of the total members have participated in the economic activities of the societies; both in women and men managed societies (Table 4.6). However, it is relatively on the higher side in women managed societies. As of attendance in the annual general body meetings, it is about 20% and 23% in women and men managed societies respectively. This may be considered as low. However, it is to be mentioned here that on an average 2–3 members are admitted from a household as members of the dairy cooperative society, and mostly the elder women/men attend the meeting and convey the resolutions taken to other members of the family. Hence low attendance

Table 4.6: Members participation in society's activities, 1993–94

Particulars	Women	Men
1. Average membership	177	257
2. Pouring members (%)	48.5	46.3
3. Attendance in general body meetings (%)	23.3	20.2
4. Members purchasing cattle feed (%)	85.4	97.5
5. Members availing AI facility (%)	100.0	85.8
6. Members insured	45.2	53.5
7. Cattle insured	50.8	43.7
8. Training programmes organised	2.3	2.7
9. People trained	69	113

Source: Records of selected societies

in general body meeting. As mentioned previously, apart from providing feed, AI, etc. the primary society also provides facilities like member insurance, cattle insurance, and organising training programmes. The status in both women and men managed societies in this respect is also presented in Table 4.6.

High percentage of non-pouring members (51–54%) is due to high rate of multiple membership from the same house which may have only one animal. The reasons for large number of multiple membership may be due to (a) eagerness to collect huge share capital, and (b) political. As of cattle feed, as many as 97.5% in men managed societies, and 85.4% in women managed societies purchased from the society. In fact this is contributing to the turnover of the society and also providing employment to a person who is looking after the distribution of cattle feed. Percentage of attendance in annual general body meetings is higher in women managed societies. Interestingly all the members in women managed societies availed the artificial insemination facilities for their animals while about 86% in men managed societies availed this facility. Similarly, 51% of the cattle in the women managed societies and 44% of the cattle in the men managed societies are insured with the help received from Amul. Same is also true with the members insured. This facility is being extended to all member societies and as many as half of the members in both the categories are covered under this scheme. In terms of training programmes organised, women managed societies performed less satisfactorily compared to their counterparts. On an average about 69 people in women managed societies and 113 persons in men managed societies were trained in 1993–94. Thus, again on the basis of majority of the qualitative parameters studied, women managed societies tend to perform better than their counterparts.

4.4 Distribution of Profit

As per the provisions of the primary cooperative society, the gross profit of the previous year shall be declared in the annual general body meeting and deductions like (a) interest payable on loans and deposits, (b) working expenses of the society, (c) losses, (d) depreciation on building and other assets, etc. The balance remaining after all deductions shall be treated as net profit. The net profit shall be distributed as (a) a sum not less than 25% shall be taken to the reserve fund, (b) 5% to the education fund, (c) shareholders dividend not exceeding 15% of the paid up share capital and the balance after all the above deductions shall be further distributed as 65% towards bonus in accordance with the value of milk supplied by the members, 10% each to the development fund, bonus to staff and charity fund, and 5% for the cooperative propaganda fund (NDDB, 1987). Thus, the primary cooperative societies have been contributing to the development of the village amenities in the above areas. The details of selected societies in this regard are given in Table 4.7. Women managed societies on an average contributed Rs. 10680 per year as against the Rs. 13680 by the men managed societies during the period 1990–94.

These amenities provided by the societies are analysed purposewise for both women and men managed societies and the data for 1993–94 are presented in Table 4.8. In women managed societies, the purposes included (a) honorarium to health worker, (b) contribution to panchayat fund, (c) purchase of ring bore (drinking water), (d) contribution to cooperative education, (e) construction of water troughs for cattle, (f) contribution to village panchayat for replacing old electric lights/tube lights, and (g) contribution to primary school to purchase books and racks. In the case of men managed societies, amenities provided included (a) repairs to approach road and contribution to primary school, (b) contribution to repair common electric motor, and (c) construction of community hall and for replacing old lights/tube lights. Thus, these societies have been providing not only continuous market for milk but also catering to the village requirements in the above areas. This lead to a gradual shift of power from village panchayats to milk societies. Panchayats started looking at milk societies for funds.

4.5 Quality of Services Provided

It is clear from the above analysis that these societies have been providing a variety of services and an attempt is made

Table 4.7: Growth in the contribution to generation of various funds, 1990–94

Fund	1989–90		1993–94		1990–94	
	Women	Men	Women	Men	Women	Men
1. Charity fund	4023	3188	3455	6528	4272	5472
2. Propaganda fund	2012	1594	1727	3264	2136	2736
3. Cattle development fund	4023	3188	3455	6528	4272	5472
Total	10058	7970	8637	16320	10680	13680

Source: Records of the selected societies

Table 4.8: Contribution to village amenities, 1993–94

Purpose	Amount (Rs.)
Women managed societies	
1. Honorarium to health worker of Tribhuvandas foundation	600
2. Contribution to village panchyat to purchase a ring bore	15,000
3. Cooperative education (members and committee members)	2,400
4. Construction of water trough for cattle	14,800
5. Contribution to village panchayat for replacing electric lights/tubes	1,000
6. Contribution to primary school	1,000
Total	34, 800
Men managed societies	
1. Contribution to primary school	5,500
2. Contribution to panchayat for purchasing a electric motor for supply of drinking water	3,500
3. Repairs to approach road	6,000
4. Construction of community hall	1,500
5. Contribution to village panchayat for replacing lights/tubelights	1,500
Total	18,000

to measure the quality of these services provided in women and men managed societies with the help of chi-square test. Services like (a) milk collection, (b) milk testing, (c) payment for milk, (d) supply of cattle feed, (e) supply of fodder seeds, (f) AI facility, (g) quality of AI services, (h) veterinary services, (i) contribution to village amenities, and (j) supply of Amul Samachar Patrika.

The results are presented in Table 4.9. There are no significant differences in the services provided by the two categories of societies and they are gender neutral. However, few exceptions noticed are (a) milk testing, (b) supply of fodder seeds, (c) quality of AI services, and (d) contribution to village amenities. Men managed societies may concentrate on these services so as to build confidence and gain member loyalty.

4.6 Employment Generation and Dairy Societies

On a crude estimate these primary societies have been providing direct employment to about four thousand people in the rural areas of Kheda district. They work as secretary, accountant, clerk, tester-cum-clerk, stockman-cum-tester, clerk cum milk collector, milk collector, nandsevak, etc. depending upon the volume of the milk procured by these societies. Thus, 3–4 local people are employed per society. The allocation of the work load for various categories of employees was clearly reported by Shah, 1991. These employees are to maintain about 39 books of accounts, some are to be filled in twice daily, daily, weekly, once in 10 days, monthly, quarterly, annual, periodic, etc.

The details of the paid employees in the selected societies are provided in Table 4.10. Women managed societies employed, on an average, 3.3 persons as against 4.3 in men managed societies. The average age of these employees worked out to be 32.7 years in women managed societies and 41.5 years in men managed societies. Caste-wise distribution of secretaries, who are key persons in running these societies, revealed that almost all of them are from dominant caste of the village. Same is true with other employees also. All the employees are literate and about 10% in women managed societies and 15% in men managed societies studied more than 11th standard and hence one can infer that they can manage institutions properly. Quite interestingly the average monthly salary per employee is higher by Rs. 115 in men managed societies while milk procurement per employee is more by 15435 litres in women managed societies. The above facts permit to conclude that women managed societies have been working more efficiently than men managed societies.

Table 4.9: Difference in members' perceptions regarding quality of services extended by society

Service and its quality	Women	Men	Absolute 'z' value
Milk collection			
(a) Regular	71	73	0.8313
(b) Not very regular	0	0	0.0000
(c) Very irregular	0	0	0.0000
(d) No opinion	4	2	0.8313
Milk testing			
(a) No malpractices	68	63	1.2284
(b) Some malpractices	2	6	1.4523
(c) Many malpractices	0	2	2.0075*
(d) No opinion	5	4	0.3436
Payment for milk			
(a) Always in time	66	63	0.7055
(b) Sometime delayed	7	9	0.5298
(c) Mostly delayed	0	0	0.0000
(d) No opinion	2	3	0.3268
Supply of cattle feed			
(a) Regular	65	56	1.7937
(b) Not very regular	6	8	0.5621
(c) Very irregular	3	6	1.0315
(d) No opinion	1	5	1.6688
Supply of fodder seeds			
(a) Regular	49	37	1.9802*
(b) Not very regular	15	25	1.8463
(c) Very irregular	10	11	0.2363
(d) No opinion	1	2	0.5877
AI facility			
(a) Regular	55	51	0.7164
(b) Not very regular	15	18	0.5571
(c) Very irregular	2	4	0.8313
(d) No opinion	3	2	0.3268
Quality of AI services			
(a) Good	45	54	1.5605
(b) Fair	20	14	1.1696
(c) Bad	15	3	3.0131**
(d) No opinion	0	4	2.0266*
Veterinary services			
(a) Regular	35	39	0.6532
(b) Not very regular	29	25	0.6811
(c) Very irregular	9	5	1.1221
(d) No opinion	2	6	1.4523

contd...

Table 4.9 contd.

Service and its quality	Women	Men	Absolute 'z' value
Contribution to village amenities			
(a) Regular	60	46	2.5128*
(b) Not very regular	12	15	0.6380
(c) Very regular	0	9	3.0928**
(d) No opinion	3	5	0.7275
Supply of Amul Samachar Patrika			
(a) Regular	33	26	0.9185
(b) Not very regular	25	27	0.3436
(c) Very irregular	13	18	1.0091
(d) No opinion	4	4	0.000

**Significant at 1% level of significance
* Significant at 5% level of significance
Source: Estimated

Table 4.10: Details of paid employees, 1993-94

Particulars	Women	Men
Average number of employees	3.3	4.3
Average age of employees	32.7	41.5
Caste-wise distribution		
(a) Secretary	Patel - 2 Kshatriya - 1	Brahmin - 1 Patel - 1 Kshatriya - 1
(b) All employees		
(1) Brahmin	0.0	15.4
(2) Patel	60.0	23.1
(3) Kshatriya	20.0	61.5
(4) Muslim	10.0	0.0
(5) Barber	10.0	0.0
Educational qualification		
(a) Illiterate	0.0	0.0
(b) Upto 5th standard	20.0	23.1
(c) 6–10th standard	70.0	61.5
(d) 11th and above	10.0	15.4
Average monthly salary (Rs.)	682.5	797.0
Average yearly milk procurement/ employee (litres)	56,365	40,930

Source: Records of selected societies

4.7 Fixed Assets of Milk Societies

All these societies studied have telephones in their premises. Three societies (2 women managed and a men managed) are located in village common buildings/rented houses. All societies have milkotester and other milk procurement equipment, furniture, etc. The details of the these fixed assets are presented in Table 4.11. Women managed societies, on an average, have fixed assets worth of Rs. 37162 as against Rs. 94158 in men managed societies. The value of fixed assets is fairly high in men managed societies due to their long existence in business.

4.8 Factors Responsible for the Success of Women Managed Societies

Based on the above analysis, one may conclude that the performance of 'all-women' dairy societies is comparatively better than men managed societies. The following factors contributed to the success of women managed societies:

(a) genetic potential of the animals in these societies is better,
(b) members are young, energetic, and innovative,
(c) unnecessary expenditure, leakages, and spoilages are minimum,
(d) efficient financial management,
(e) women are familiar with all operations involved in dairy farming.

Table 4.11: Details of fixed assets, 1993–94

Assets	Women	Men
Furniture	12701 (34.18)	14281 (15.17)
Building	6900 (18.57)	60945 (64.73)
Equipment	16844 (45.33)	18415 (19.56)
Others	717 (1.92)	517 (0.54)
Total	37162	94158

(Figures in parenthesis indicate percentages to total)
Source: Records of selected societies

(f) higher degree of involvement in the business activities of the society,
(g) frequency of interactions with the officials of Amul is more and thus availed all the facilities,
(h) support from family members,
(i) desire to develop a successful model dairy society, and
(j) women worked together better than men.

4.9 Summary

These dairy societies are managed by a nine member management committee and the day to day operations are looked after by paid staff comprising a secretary, milk collector, tester, etc. Physical and financial performance indicators studied included membership, milk collection, average per member contribution, sour milk, net profit, cost of procurement, etc. When measured on the above parameters, women managed societies fared relatively better during the study period (1990–94). Men managed societies realised better price as they maintained mostly buffaloes. Rate of conception (%) is better in women managed societies and hence they are happy with the quality of AI services provided by the union. Similarly, women managed societies did well in providing milk production enhancement inputs too. As of management committee, involvement of women members in terms of number of meetings conducted, average attendance, frequency of interaction with officials of Amul, etc. is again on the higher side. There is a gradual shift of power from village panchayats to milk societies. Both categories of societies contributed to the village amenities. Average monthly salary/employee is less in women managed societies but the average milk procurement/employee is more. Because of their long existence, men managed societies have more fixed assets. As regards quality of services provided, there are no significant differences in opinion of the members. On the basis of above findings, factors responsible for the success of women managed societies are identified.

5

Status of Women

An attempt is made in this chapter to understand the status of women during pre and post enrolment in the dairy society. Status is analysed in terms of participation in activities related to household, agriculture, and dairying, decision making process, and recognition in house and society.

5.1 Basis of Sexual Division of Labour

Women's role in rural development has been focus of attention of researchers since the publication of Easter Boserup's classic book 'women's role in economic development' in 1970. Boserup argued that while modernisation of agriculture in Sub-Saharan Africa had drawn men into commodity production, it had worsened the position of women who lost their informal rights to land. Boserup went on saying that with the transition from subsistence to cash economy, women's role changed from a decision maker/cultivator to that of family aid or hired hand. Division of labour among sexes depends on the gender related issues. According to Ruben (1975), gender is the set of arrangements by which a society transforms biological sexuality into products of human activity and in which these transformed sexual needs are satisfied. Goetz (1991) opined that 'gender refers to the socially constructed and institutionalised forms of identity which are attached to biological sex differences, and gendering is the process of producing these forms, through the granting or withholding of significant social, political, and economic resources. Gender is a neutral term and age, economic stratification, cultural and religious beliefs are all important factors in determining the nature of gender relations at the local level'. Gender is a basic element in the individual's self concept. The knowledge of maleness or femaleness of the individual is acquired in life. The treatment received by and the role and responsibilities assigned to the individual by the family members is also dependent on the gender difference. These differences in treatment between sexes are intensified by adolescence, and contribute to stable mental and behavioural sex differences and forms the basis of sexual division of labour (Datta, Das, and Basu, 1995). In the light of above observations, an attempt is made here to identify the women's participation in household, agriculture and animal husbandry. Assuming that the degree of participation of women in the above three activities varies depending upon the involvement, four levels of participation are identified: (a) regular, (b) occasional, (c) very irregular, and (d) not at all.

5.1.1 Female labour participation

Questions pertaining to women in labour force in India engaged the attention of prospective scholars like Dr. Gadgil as early as 1924 (Gadgil, 1938). Publication of the Labour Bureaus 'Economic and Social Status of Workers in India' focussed attention on the legislative measures for protection and welfare of women employment, male-female differentials in wages and earnings, working conditions, etc. for the period ending 1950. It has been said that women are invisible workers. The invisibility thrust is upon them by confining them to the so called subordinate roles.

Society needs both men and women. There are certain activities attended to mostly by men while there are some requiring the involvement of women. In general, arduous tasks like ploughing, threshing, application of fertilizers, irrigating crops, etc. are attended to by men, while activities like seed bed preparation, sowing, transplantation, weeding, harvesting, winnowing, etc. are attended to by women. Thus, there exists a clear cut division of agricultural activities between the sexes.

Female labour participation in 3 major sectors (ie) household, agriculture, and animal husbandry is given in Table 5.1. Average/day hours spent in all 3 sectors is 12.5 hours before enrolment in the society and it increased to 16 hours a day after enrolment. Thus, there is an increase of 35% of work per woman/day. The time spent per woman/day in the household activities accounted for 46.9% of a total time spent during the post enrolment period. Next in the order is time spent on animal husbandry activities which comes to around 6.4 hours a day. Surprisingly, there is a substantial decline in the time spent by women in agriculture sector in the post enrolment period. The time withdrawn from agriculture allowed them to concentrate more on animal husbandry and household activities. Thus, women spent more time in the house in the post enrolment vis-a-vis pre enrolment in dairy society.

It has been reported that there are variations in the wages paid to men and women across various activities performed by both the sexes. With a view to understand the existing wage rates, and wage differentials among male and female labourers relevant data are presented in Table 5.2. Surprisingly no male-female wage differentials are observed in the study area. Similar results were also reported by Spodek (1994)

Table 5.1: Distribution of female labour hours in various activities during pre and post enrolment in dairy society (per day)

Sector	Pre enrolment	Post enrolment	Difference
Household	5.5 (44.0)	7.5 (46.9)	+ 2.0
Agriculture	3.5 (28.0)	2.1 (13.1)	– 1.4
Animal husbandry	3.5 (28.0)	6.4 (40.0)	+ 2.9
Total	12.5 (100.0)	16.0 (100.0)	+ 3.5

Note: An analysis of female labour hours in mixed gender societies revealed lower levels of participation by women. On an average women worked for 10 hours during pre enrolment and 12 hours during post enrolment period.

Source: Field study

for Gujarat, and NCSEWWIS (1988) for Himachal Pradesh. Across various activities considered, wage rates for transplantation is the highest, Rs. 17 per day. Apart from these monetary wages, labourers are also given one time meal (either chapaties and/or rice with one curry), 2 teas, and 3 beedies. Only difference in wages across sexes is that most of the women are non-smokers thus they could not get the beedies. Also while coming from the farm they are free to carry head load of green fodder. As women are relatively physically weak compared to men they brought less quantity of fodder. As of tending cattle, wages are on monthly basis and mostly old and handicapped people attended to this work. These people tend animals along road sides and on the village common lands for about 4–5 hours a day and bring them back to the respective households.

5.1.2 Participation of women in agriculture

Female labour participation in agricultural activities is presented in Table 5.3. It is evident from the table that there are certain activities where women are participating 'regularly' and to some extent 'occasionally'. Most interestingly, in all the 12 activities considered the participation of women has declined as a result of enrolment in the dairy society. Women are predominantly involved in transplantation/seed sowing, weeding, harvesting, and winnowing and cleaning produce. The findings of this study are corroborated by Dak, Sharma, and Jain (1986), and Tantray (1991) on participation of women

Table 5.2: Prevailing average wage rates in the study area, 1995

Activities	Women	Men
	(Rupees per day)	
Transplantation	17.00	17.00
Weeding	14.50	14.50
Harvesting	16.50	16.50
Winnowing and cleaning	16.00	16.00
Cutting and bringing grass	8.00	8.00*
Tending cattle	12.00	12.00**

* This work is only for 3.5–4 hours a day
** The wage rate is on monthly basis
Source: Field study

Table 5.3: Female labour participation in agriculatural activities during pre and post enrolment

Activity	Regular		Occasional		Very irregular		Not at all		Paired 't' Value
	Pre	Post	Pre	Post	Pre	Post	Pre	Post	
Field preparation	0	0	19	0	51	35	5	40	7.9105**
Transplantation/ seed sowing	46	5	20	36	4	27	5	7	12.6811**
Making farm yard manure	0	0	44	38	29	28	2	9	2.7248**
Carrying inputs to field	0	0	21	0	52	11	2	64	15.8326**
Manure/fertilizer application	0	0	8	0	33	4	34	71	8.1633**
Irrigation crops	0	0	5	0	34	10	36	65	6.1452**
Construction/ repair field channels	0	0	0	0	21	8	54	67	3.9386**
Weeding	36	27	26	37	9	8	4	4	6.5750**
Harvesting	34	21	26	15	15	29	0	0	5.7350**
Threshing	0	0	0	0	42	25	33	50	12.7254**
Winnowing & cleaning	42	24	15	12	14	35	4	4	6.0025**
Transporting produce	0	0	10	5	35	20	30	50	3.1576**

** Significant at 1% level of significance
Source: Field study

in farm activities. Their participation in other activities considered are either 'irregular' or 'not at all'. It could be due to their engagement in other activities like household and animal husbandry. The difference between the pre and post enrolment in the society is tested with the help of paired 't' test and it is highly significant in all the activities considered [for more details on paired 't' test, see Walpole (1968)].

5.1.3 *Participation of women in dairying*

Subsequently an attempt is also made to observe the changes in the female labour participation in animal husbandry activities during pre and post enrolment period and the details are given in Table 5.4. Activities considered are (a) tending cattle, (b) bringing fodder, (c) feeding animals, (d) watering animals, (e) milking, (f) taking milk to society, (g) cleaning utensils, (h) cleaning cattleshed, (i) removing dung, and (j) preparing dung cakes.

By tradition, work related to dairying is considered as the sole responsibility of women/daughters in the study area. Women members hesitate to assign this work to men/sons and majority of them felt that men should not attend to this work. Female labour participation in activities related to dairying have not undergone significant changes as a result of enrolment in the society (Table 5.4). As a matter of fact women devoted more time to this avocation compared to earlier period. As of female work efficiency, it has been reported by as many as 93% of respondents that women are the most suitable for milking animals as their hands are tender. Similar opinion is expressed for activities like feeding, and preparing dung cakes. There is a sharp decline in the number of women taking animals for tending, bringing fodder from fields, while the number of women taking milk to society showed a substantial increase in the post enrolment period. Thus, increasing participation of women in dairying accompanied by withdrawal of men may lead to a process of 'feminisation of dairy labour force'. Paired 't' test indicated significant differences in female labour participation in only three activities after enrolment.

5.2 Decision making by Women

The family's decision making process is implicit in all its distribution of responsibilities and resources. The most powerful family member is determined by prevailing cultural values, such as those attached to old age, sex, and the relative importance attached to men's and women's productive role (Charlton, 1984). Further, level of education, exposure to developmental activities, media, etc. will also be counted. In a society like ours, women are generally not expected to be self-supporting, have few opportunities to earn significant incomes, and generally cannot inherit land or other property. It is said that the failure to involve women in the decision making about the new technology meant that several factors crucial to the usefulness of the technology were overlooked.

5.2.1 Decision making in household

While considering the process of decision making in the house-

Table 5.4: Female labour participation in animal husbandry activities during pre and post enrolment

Activity	Regular		Occasional		Very irregular		Not at all		Paired 't' Value
	Pre	Post	Pre	Post	Pre	Post	Pre	Post	
Tending cattle	10	4	15	13	34	33	29	35	3.7654 **
Bringing fodder	40	32	15	18	12	15	8	10	1.7854 *
Feeding animals	63	59	8	12	4	4	0	0	2.6240 **
Watering animals	54	55	15	20	6	0	0	0	1.2345
Milking	60	69	10	6	5	0	0	0	1.5469
Taking milk to society	12	40	25	28	18	7	20	0	4.9567 **
Cleaning utensils	55	54	16	17	4	4	0	0	1.0579
Cleaning cattleshed	20	20	26	29	17	21	12	5	1.2959
Removing dung	25	30	29	32	12	3	9	0	1.5629
Preparing dung cakes	36	31	20	25	15	16	4	3	1.4297

** Significant at 1% level of significance
* Significant at 5% level of significance
Source: Field study

hold, agriculture, and animal husbandry an attempt is made to study the nature and power achieved or authority exercised by women. Authority, as defined by Leacock (1986), is influenced and exerted through recognized channels. Operationalization of decision making is done through women's perception as to who mainly decides and controls the family in particular activity. It is hypothesized that the level of participation in the decision making will improve during post enrolment because of economic and political empowerment. Decision making by the sample women in household activities is given in Table 5.5.

The data on female participation in decision making at home indicated that men took decisions pertaining to casting vote, investment in shares, purchase of durable consumer

Table 5.5: Participation of women in decision making process in household related activities.

Activity	Women only		Men only		Both		Paired 't' value
	Pre	Post	Pre	Post	Pre	Post	
Child bearing	20	25	20	10	35	40	2.3456**
Children's education	5	15	25	17	45	43	1.9751**
Treatment to children	5	15	25	17	43	43	6.7291**
Purchase of clothes	15	35	14	10	46	30	3.5428**
Purchase of jewellary	8	18	35	22	32	35	2.1308**
Children's marriage	7	10	28	15	40	50	1.7209*
Taking/giving loan	3	9	55	32	17	34	1.5298
Purchase of durable consumer goods	4	20	45	24	26	31	4.5092**
Investment in shares	0	3	55	45	20	27	1.2351
Casting vote	2	20	55	25	18	30	2.0521**

** Significant at 1% level of significance
* Significant at 5% level of significance
Source: Field study

goods, taking/giving loans, and purchase of jewellery during the pre-enrolment in society. The decision in the rest of the activities is taken by both women and men combined. Age at the time of marriage of respondents studies hovered around 15–17 years which is less than the minimum age prescribed for marriage. This suggests that respondents had little choice when they were young. However, there is a substantial improvement in the decision making by women after enrolment in the society. It is evident in all the activities considered. Improvement in the decision making can be attributed to their economic and political empowerment.

5.2.2 Decision making in agriculture and animal husbandry

Similarly, an attempt is also made to understand the participation of women in decision making in agriculture and animal husbandry activities (Table 5.6). Men dominated the decision making in all the activities related to agriculture while women took decisions pertaining to animal husbandry. Moreover, there is a shift towards women's participation after the enrolment. Thus, it is evident from Tables 5.5, and 5.6 that

Table 5.6: Participation of women in decision making process in agriculture and animal husbandry activities.

Decision	Women only		Men only		Both		Paired 't' value
	Pre	Post	Pre	Post	Pre	Post	
Choice of crops	4	10	35	18	36	47	2.1175**
Area under crops	0	3	51	37	24	35	1.7215 *
Seed Selection	0	4	49	35	26	36	1.9574**
Use of/ manures fertilizers	0	2	45	30	30	43	1.5632
Purchase/sale of land	2	6	28	19	45	50	1.2545
Breeding activities	12	15	20	11	43	49	6.5371**
Feeding activities	22	39	19	12	34	24	12.3579**
Fodder cultivation	9	13	36	25	30	37	4.5390**
Health and disease control	10	18	45	37	20	20	1.9218**
Management activities	6	25	42	14	27	36	8.9543**
Purchase/sale of milch cattle	11	31	24	5	40	39	7.2555**
Purchase/sale	0	0	50	45	25	30	1.3545

** Significant at 1% level of significance
* Significant at 5% level of significance
Source: Field Study

women actively participated in decision making in majority of the activities considered. The above data also shows that sample respondents have been participating in the decision making at relatively higher levels than some of the earlier studies (Shobha 1987, and Sethi, 1991).

The findings of the present study are at variance with the results reported by Mitra's study on women in dairying in Andhra Pradesh (Mitra, 1984). Mitra concluded that introduction of dairying among landless and poor peasants has increased woman's workload without giving them adequate access to the fruits of their labour, or to new avenues of participation and management of the dairy cooperatives. Similar results were also reported by Mies, Lalita, and Kumari, 1986. However, Tripathi and Arya (1994) reported higher levels of participation in decision making pattern of farm women in animal husbandry enterprise. Household decision making is also associated with land size, caste of respondents, and education. The women of high caste hindu families exerted more power in decision making than low caste hindu families. Similarly, educated women participated actively than their illiterate counterparts. These women are fully involved in all the activities related to dairying and the new technology is introduced only when the women are convinced about it. Thus, the results corroborates the findings of Whyte (1982) wherein it was stated that 'women's contribution to family income is critical for estimates of market response and for reaction to policy changes or economic and financial decisions'.

5.3 Status of Women

Participation in decision making may lead to expectations for higher social status. The urge for higher social status is perhaps the beginning for social development and cultural changes. If supported adequately by larger social and political milieu, such urge becomes realities paving the way for a better society.

Keeping it in mind the women respondents are asked to indicate their status in the house and in the society after joining dairy society. Status is measured on a 3 point scale ranging from 0–3 and the respondents are asked to indicate the level of improvement in their status after joining the society and details are presented, land-wise, in Table 5.7. It is very interesting to observe that about 29% of the women have opined that their status has 'substantially improved' after joining society. Similarly, about 47% of them have indicated that their status has 'improved'. Similar experiences were also reported by Nagabrahmam (1987) in parts of Andhra Pradesh and Gujarat. However, there are 4 respondents with small land holdings who opined that their status has 'decreased' after joining society. It is to be mentioned here that these 4 respondents hails from drought prone village of the sample and are belonging to Kshatriya community. All the 4 took loans from a bank and purchased milch animals. Unfortunately the animals were dead. Since insurance policy was not renewed in the subsequent years the policy was lapsed and as a result they could not get the indemnity from the insurance company. Thus, they faced a number of problems in repaying the loan to the bank.

Table 5.7: Respondents' opinion about increase/decrease in their status

Land holding(ha)	Substantially improved	Improved	No Change	Decreased	Total
Landless	1	2	3	0	6
	(16.7)	(33.3)	(50.0)	(0.0)	(100.0)
Small	10	21	9	4	44
(ha 0.1–2.0)	(22.7)	(47.7)	(20.5)	(9.1)	(100.0)
Medium	7	12	2	0	21
(ha 2.1–4.0)	(33.3)	(57.2)	(9.5)	(0.0)	(100.0)
Large	4	0	0	0	4
(ha 4.1 and above)	(100.0)	(0.0)	(0.0)	(0.0)	(100.0)
Total	22	35	14	4	75
	(29.3)	(46.7)	(18.7)	(5.3)	(100.0)

(Figures in parentheses are percentages to total)
Source: Field study

5.4 Summary

Female labour participation in household, agriculture, and animal husbandry activities revealed that on an average, women worked for 16 hours/day during the post enrolment period, their work increased by 3.5 hours/day during this period. Across various sectors, their participation declined in agriculture while that in household, and dairying increased. Participation of women in decision making in agriculture and dairying indicated that there is significant improvement in decision making, more so in dairying, during the post enrolment period. Respondents from landed households, high caste hindu families with higher education exerted more power than others. As of status of women, 76% of the respondents have indicated that it has increased, while only 5% opined that it has decreased. Unlike the observations of Sharma and Vanjani (1989). 'All women' dairy cooperatives in the study area provided necessary training, arranged credit and technical support, and won their confidence which resulted in improved economic and social status of women.

6

Effectiveness of Cooperative Education

An attempt is made in this chapter to assess the effectiveness of training programmes conducted by Amul, and to identify the key areas for future training programmes.

6.1 Importance of Training

Training is a process of learning a sequence of programmed behaviour. It is an application of knowledge which gives people an awareness of the rules and procedures to guide their behaviour. The benefits of training will extend throughout a person's career and may help to develop that person for future responsibilities. The objective of the training should be to impart such knowledge, develop such attitude, cultivate such skills as may help the participant to improve his/her performance on the work and thereby help to contribute to the overall improvement in the enterprise.

6.1.1 Cooperative development programme

NDDB initiated a Cooperative Development (CD) programme in 1989 to promote and support self reliant, autonomous, member owned and controlled cooperatives. The focus of the programme is to bring about increased member participation in cooperative business activities, making the cooperatives strong viable business enterprises responsive to the needs of the members (for more details on CD programme, see NDDB, 1993, 1994b, and 1994c). After studying several successful models of cooperative education and member relations around the world, NDDB identified four instruments to address awareness, role perception and motivation of (a) members, (b) managing committees and boards, (c) professionals and staff, and (d) the social, economic and political environment (NDDB, 1989). In each union a team of five educators/trainers, consisting of a Coordinator (Institutional Development Officer), two women and two men instructors, conducts a variety of educational and training activities. The CD group at the union is headed by an Institutional Development Officer (IDO), who is in the rank of Deputy Manager. IDO is assisted by 4 female and 4 male instructors. All the 4 male instructors are veterinarians, two of women instructors are post graduates, while the rest completed their graduation. Entire team is divided into two groups. Based on the needs, month-wise calendar is prepared and programmes for leadership development, committee members training, etc. are being conducted. In order to facilitate the working of group members, two vehicles are put at their disposal. On an average, they cover 100 societies in a year.

Realising the important role played by women, the CD programme has focussed its attention on 'women education programme' and on encouragement of women leaders. The objective of this programme is to provide knowledge about the functioning of cooperative society, benefits of dairy cooperative, women's role in a cooperative, management of milch animals and clean milk production, human nutrition, health care, etc. It is a three day programme organised in the village for 2–3 hour for the first two days followed by field visit to Anand on the third day. The progress of the union in organising such programmes was given in chapter 2.

6.1.2 *Attitudes towards training*

In order to assess the impact of CD programme, NDDB has conducted studies in a number of participating unions. These results revealed that the CD women's education programme has been reasonably effective in conveying information on cooperation, member's role, and women's roles specially, as well as promoting positive attitudes towards cooperative societies and toward exercising the rights and responsibilities of members.

With a view to elicit the respondents opinion, women respondents are asked to express their attitude towards training and the responses are measured on a 4 point scale: 0 strongly disagree; 1 disagree; 2 cannot say; 3 agree; and 4 strongly agree and the results are presented in Table 6.1.

Average score noticed for the statement 'skills related to dairying are inborn and training does not make difference' is 2.44 which is in between 'cannot say' and 'agree'. Thus, one can easily conclude that the respondents realised the importance of training in this sector. Similar is true with other three statements also. The highest average score (2.8) obtained for the statement 'training imparts knowledge and methods regarding scientific milk production' also corroborates the above findings.

Table 6.1: Women respondents' attitude towards training

Parameter	Scale										Average score
	0	%	1	%	2	%	3	%	4	%	
A	5	6.7	10	13.3	16	21.3	35	46.7	9	12.0	2.44
B	7	9.3	11	14.7	20	26.7	19	25.3	18	24.0	2.40
C	15	20.0	14	18.6	11	14.7	20	26.6	15	20.0	2.08
D	4	5.3	7	9.3	25	33.3	22	29.3	17	22.7	2.79

A = Skills related to dairying are inborn and training does not make any difference

B = Skills related to dairying are learnt from parents/neighbourers since childhood and training makes little difference

C = Individuals learn more from education than attending training programmes

D = Training imparts knowledge and methods regarding scientific milk production.

Score

0 = Strongly disagree
1 = Disagree
2 = Cannot say
3 = Agree
4 = Strongly agree

Source: Field study

As to understand the respondents opinion about efforts made by Amul in imparting training to its member producers, women respondents are asked to give their opinion on five statements related to training efforts of Amul. These results are presented in Table 6.2. It can be noticed from Table 6.2 that the average score ranged between 2.15 and 2.61 indicating a positive opinion of the respondents towards efforts of Amul. Interestingly, average score obtained for the statement 'efforts are being made to develop women leaders', is 2.61 which is falling between 'true' and 'true to great extent'. Amul has to be appreciated for realising the importance of women and its efforts to develop leadership qualities among them. Such an effort will go a long way in bringing more women to the mainstream and in the process of decision making. Average score reported, (2.15), for the statement 'women trainers are knowledgable and cooperative' appears to be on the lower side. Necessary training and motivation

6.2: Women respondents' opinion about training efforts of Amul

Parameter	Scale										Average score
	0	%	1	%	2	%	3	%	4	%	
A	9	12.0	13	17.4	18	24.0	21	28.0	14	18.6	2.24
*B	5	9.4	2	3.8	30	56.6	12	22.6	4	7.6	2.15
*C	2	3.8	2	3.8	27	50.9	15	28.3	7	13.2	2.43
*D	3	5.7	4	7.5	26	49.1	11	20.8	9	16.9	2.36
E	5	6.7	8	10.7	14	18.7	32	42.7	16	21.2	2.61

* Opinion on these statements are elicited from those participants who had undergone training earlier.

A = Amul genuinely believes that training of women in dairy activities is extremely useful

B = Women trainers are knowledgeable and cooperative

C = Participants skills/knowledge is given due recognition in training programmes

D = Efforts are made to provide training again

E = Efforts are being made to develop women leaders

Score

0 = Not true at all

1 = Somewhat true

2 = True

3 = True to a great extent

4 = Very true

Source: Field study

may be given to those trainers working sincerely in the rural areas with a cause to develop the human resources of the village women.

6.1.3 Training programmes attended by women producers

All the three women managed societies are covered under CD programme and the details of the women undergone training during the last five years are provided in Table 6.3. Of the 75 respondents, as many as 71% attended the women's education programme. There is positive correlation between land holdings and number of training programmes attended during the last five years. On an average, they attended 2–3 training programmes during the study period. Low levels of income, illiteracy, and ignorance about the training programmes may be responsible for their low participation in training programmes by landless households. The union should take necessary steps to provide training facilities to all the members without any bias. Such an arrangement will make the members loyal to union and help members in increasing quality milk production by utilizing all services provided by the union.

6.1.4 Effectiveness of training on women

Apart from the imparting training on human nutrition and health care, and benefits of dairy cooperative society; CD

Table 6.3: Training programme attended by women dairy farmers

Land holding (ha)	Total	Women trained	Average number of programmes
Landless	6 (8.00)	3 (5.66)	1.5
Small (0.1-2.0)	44 (58.67)	30 (56.60)	2.3
Medium (2.1-4.0)	21 (28.00)	16 (30.19)	2.4
Large (4.1 and above)	4 (5.33)	4 (7.55)	2.8
Total	75 (100.00)	53 (100.00)	2.3

Source: Field study

group impart training on scientific milk production including breeding, feeding, health care, and general management. The effectiveness of the training programmes on these broad categories are analysed and presented in Table 6.4. Since, these opinions vary according to economic status and land holding, respondents are categorised land-wise and responses are measured on a three point scale ranging from 1–3. Of the 3 landless respondents who have undergone training, two indicated that training has 'improved' their knowledge in cattle breeding. As of respondents of small holdings, 18 have indicated

Table 6.4: Effectiveness of training on women dairy farmers

Training	Landless	Small (ha 0.1–2.0)	Medium (ha 2.1–4.0)	Large (ha 4.1 and above)	Total
1. Cattle breeding					
(a) Substantially improved	0	5	4	2	11
(b) Improved	2	18	9	2	31
(c) No change	1	4	2	0	7
(d) No opinion	0	3	1	0	4
(e) Total	3	30	16	4	53
2. Feeding					
(a) Substantially improved	0	0	1	1	2
(b) Improved	0	9	6	3	18
(c) No change	2	15	5	0	22
(d) No opinion	1	6	4	0	11
(e) Total	3	30	16	4	53
3. Health care					
(a) Substantially improved	0	2	3	1	6
(b) Improved	1	15	8	3	27
(c) No change	2	8	2	0	12
(d) No opinion	0	5	3	0	8
(e) Total	3	30	16	4	53
4. General management					
(a) Substantially improved	1	8	6	2	17
(b) Improved	2	19	10	2	33
(c) No change	0	3	0	0	3
(d) No opinion	0	0	0	0	0
(e) Total	3	30	16	4	53

Source: Field study

that their skills have improved as a result of training and 5 respondents indicated that their knowledge substantially improved. Similar responses are observed from respondents from medium and large holdings. Thus, there is a positive correlation between land holdings and effectiveness of training programmes on breeding. Similar is the case with feeding, health care, and general management. As many as 32% of the respondents have indicated that their knowledge in general management of animal husbandry activities has improved substantially as a result of training programmes, and another 62% of respondents indicated that knowledge has 'improved' because of the training programmes. Thus, it is clear from the above table that training has improved the knowledge of dairy farmers on scientific milk production.

6.2 Requirement for Additional Topics

While the above table revealed about the opinion of respondents regarding the effectiveness of training programmes, an attempt is also made to elicit additional topics required by women respondents (Table 6.5). Landless households listed (a) family planning, (b) child care, (c) clean milk production, and sanitation as important areas where they need additional information. Quite interestingly, the priorities have changed across the land holdings. In the case of respondents from small holdings, priorities included child care, clean milk production, watershed management, crop cultivation, and sanitation in that order. It is a fact that the study villages are located in water scarce areas and the farmers having small land are more interested in watershed management and crop cultivation, improved agronomic practices which will help improving profits as well as availability of fodder, and this is reflected in the priorities indicated by women farmers. Similarly, respondents of medium holdings required additional information on watershed management, leadership development, sanitation, and crop cultivation. Thus, one can see that the need for leadership development programmes is expressed by the respondents of medium households thereby indicating their interest in managing business enterprises and thus, entering other national programmes. In the case of large farmers, train-

Table 6.5 : Respondents' requirement for additional topics

Land holding (ha)	Additional topics
Landless	(1) Family planning (2) Child care (3) Clean milk production (4) Sanitation
Small (0.1–2.0)	(1) Child care (2) Clean milk production (3) Watershed management (4) Crop cultivation (5) Sanitation
Medium	(1) Watershed management (2) Leadership development (3) Sanitation (4) Crop cultivation
Large	(1) Leadership development (2) Book keeping (3) Financial management (4) Heat detection (5) Animal nutrition

Source: Field study

ing programmes on leadership development, book keeping, financial management, heat detection, and animal nutrition are sought. Thus, leadership development programmes and the management of cooperative institutions are the important topics of interest to the respondents of medium and large size holdings while it is child care, clean milk production and family planning to the small and landless households. Management of Amul may make necessary arrangements to include these topics in the curriculum of training programmes and identify target group such that respondents' priorities are met.

6.2.1 Opinion about future training programmes

An attempt is also made to elicit respondents' interest about the conduct of future training programmes. Of the 75 respondents as many as 57% have opted to attend programmes outside their village and the rest preferred to attend programmes in the village itself (Table 6.6). The percentage of respondents who opted to attend programmes outside village are more in large, medium, and small holdings in that order. As regards

Table 6.6: Respondents' opinion about future training programmes

Opinion	Landless	Small (ha 0.1–2.0)	Medium (ha 2.1–4.0)	Large (ha 4.1 and above)
1. Like to attend the programmes outside the village:				
Yes	0	24	15	4
No	6	20	6	0
2. Preference to the sex of trainers:				
Women	6	19	11	4
Men	0	8	5	0
Both	0	17	5	0
3. Average duration of the programme (days)	2.3	3.5	3.0	3.2
4. Ability to train others				
Yes	2	28	18	4
No	4	16	4	0

Source: Field study

preference to the sex of trainers, more than 50% of them preferred women trainers, 17% shown their interest towards men trainers while the rest opted for both the sexes. Thus, it can be concluded that majority of the respondents are willing to have women trainers and Amul may arrange training programmes specially by women trainers. The average duration of the training programme as mentioned by the respondents is about 3 days and it ranged between 2.3 days in landless households to 3.5 days in respondents of small holdings. Thus, existing 3 days duration programme appears to be reasonable. As of their convenience to attend programmes, about 72% of them indicated April–May while rest were willing to attend the programme in any month. Respondents are also asked to express their capacity to train other members of the village after undergoing a training programme and about 69% of them gave a positive answer to the above to the above statement and the percentage of people who expressed their ability to train are more in large, medium, and small holdings.

6.3 Summary

The study of the effectiveness of training programmes indicated that majority of respondents are interested in undergoing training programmes and also they are aware of the effectiveness and utility of the programmes. About 71% of the respondents interviewed are trained during the last 5 years and their ability with regard to breeding, feeding, health care, and general management has fairly increased as a result of training programmes. As regards future training requirements respondents of landless and small holdings indicated family planning, child care, and clean milk production as their priorities, while leadership development, and crop cultivation were indicated by medium and large holdings. Majority of the respondents have shown their willingness to attend training programme of about 3 days duration outside the village and would like to have training from women trainers.

7

Women Dairy Farmers Profiles

While the results provided in the previous chapters dealt with averages, an attempt is made here to provide selected individual case studies interviewed during data collection. Choice of the particular individual is based on cooperation, uniqueness, caste, region, articulation, etc. which helped in developing a detailed exposition of the individual. In all, 12 such cases are documented in this chapter and some of the names given in the case studies are fictitious.

7.1 Sarayuben Patel (28 years): She is the Chairman of primary dairy cooperative society and chosen for a detailed case study as she appeared to be cooperative, articulate, and ambitious. Sarayuben studied upto 10th standard and got married at the age of 18. She hails from a nearby village where she has two sisters and a brother, all of them studied upto 12th standard and belongs to a farming community. When there was a move to organise 'all-women' dairy cooperative society, menfolk recommended her name because (a) she hails from a high caste hindu family which is also a majority community in the village, (b) she hails from landed household, (c) she is educated, and (d) she is highly articulate. Her day starts at 5.00 am with supervising the activities like cleaning shed, watering animals, and feeding animals. They have a hired labour to look after the animals. However, she milks all the four crossbred cows and is of the opinion that 'woman's fingers are tender than men's and hence the udder may not get hurt'. It takes 40 minutes for her to complete this work. As her mother-in-law looks after the household chores, she takes milk to the society and sits there for two and a half to three hours till the milk truck comes at 8.00 am. In her opinion, her presence is essential as to provide moral boost to women employees, and also to keep a watch on the activities of the society. Since the society is in infant stage, it is located in the village building. She is getting cooperation from all members of the society. Further, she is supported by husband, in-laws and children.

7.2 Kankuben Sumabai: Frail, dark complexioned and wizend, seventy-two-years old Kankuben belongs to Vankar (scheduled caste) community and is one of the founder members of the society. She has three sons and three daughters and all of them are married. Her husband died at the age of 41 and she toiled to feed the children and get them married. She has constructed two houses for the two sons and the younger one is staying with her. She has two buffaloes, both purchased from bank loan, and a male and female calf. As the village is located in drought prone area, she depends wholly on the income from milk. Buffaloes are in milk at the time of interview (February–April) and selling 3 litres of milk in the morning and 2 litres in the evening. She retains 750 ml for home consumption. She gets Rs. 400–425 for 10 days of which Rs. 85 is spent on cattle feed which is purchased from the milk society. As they are landless, she also spends Rs. 35–40 on dry fodder and collects green fodder from 'others' fields. Since it is a dry land area, getting green fodder, except in the monsoon, is very difficult. There is acute drinking water problem in the village. The milk society constructed two water troughs to cater to the water requirements of the cattle. However, the water supplied through the village water works comes only for 30–40 minutes in the summer thus, collecting little water in the troughs. She is of opinion that the things are much better than before the establishment of milk society. She carried milk, both times, for 2 km round the year and narrated the difficulties encountered. As of her status in the village, after joining the society, she unequivocally mentioned that it has substantially increased. She can walk in the village streets without inhibition, stand before/after any high caste hindu community person at the milk society, particularly in the society's annual general meeting. She believes in artificial insemination and need for balanced cattle feed. Though she had six children, she succeeded in convincing all her children to undergo tubectomy. Now that she has completed her all responsibilities, she wants to purchase 3 bicycles for her sons-in-law. She is very much engrossed in rearing cattle and bringing up her children. Though, she is aware of the benefits of the crossbred cows, lack of green fodder, water, space and capital came in her way in rearing them. Self contented Kankuben's access to the income and self determination has made her not only more important in the house but also in the village. Last year her youngest daughter got married and she gave a 'payal' set (anklet), a gold ring of 5 grams, utensils, dress material and Rs. 5000 as dowry. The marriage costed her about Rs. 10000 of which Rs. 3000 were borrowed from villagers. Rest of money was generated out of milk business. She is confident of repaying the loan in a year's time. She believes in optimum utilization of time and feels that the society in which we are brought up plays a vital role in shaping our personality.

7.3 Jubedadidi Isumiya (38 years): Jubedadidi is the chairwoman of cooperative milk society. The village is located in a rainfed area of the district. She has two sons and three daughters and all of them are going to school located in the village. They have 3 acres of dry land, two buffaloes and a female calf. Though, she studied upto 2nd standard, she got the chairwomanship by sheer majority of her community in the village. Prior to becoming chairwoman, she was on the board for 9 years which also helped her to get this post. This milk society is first ever 'all women' society formed in Kaira district way back in 1968. They have two horses which are used in marriages and for special functions and fetche premium wages in marriage season. The total milk production, as on the date of interview, is 8 litres of which 1.5 litres is retained and 6.5 litres sold to the milk society. An amount of Rs. 12 was spent per animal on dry fodder, Amul concentrate, and groundnut cake which is purchased from the open market. She earns a net income of Rs. 700–750 in a month which is sufficient to maintain her family. They are fully dependent on the income from milk only as income from horses is seasonal, and income from dry land is uncertain. Whatsoever income is generated out of two activities is considered as saving to the family.

She is not fully equipped with the knowledge required for running an enterprise. Though she brought milk to the society, she took little interest in the activities of the society. As of status of women in the society, she feels that 'in a home context a man could be traumatised by a woman. But it is different in the work context. She is also of the opinion that women have been known to be seductresses. In that process, they can never be aggressive'. When asked about the problems in running the society, she mentioned that there are a number of communities in the village and it is difficult to satisfy all requirements of the villagers. Major problems facing the village are: (a) acute shortage of water, for both people and animals. (b) shortage of green fodder, (c) poverty, and (d) illiteracy.

She has not attended any training programme and her husband is also not very keen in sending her out for training. Her female children help her in the household chores and also in keeping the animals but no help from sons and husband. When asked about the computerisation of records in the society, she likes it provided machinery and necessary training required are given free of cost by Amul.

7.4 Chandrikaben (30 years): Hardworking, young, energetic, articulate and enthusiastic, Chandrikaben belongs to Patel community. She studied upto 10th standard and got married at the age of 19. She has two sisters and two brothers who are staying 8 km away from her in-laws village. Being the youngest in the family, she studied the maximum in the house. Immediately after the marriage she came to her husband's house which is a joint family. She has two sons, a daughter and has undergone tubectomy.

Prior to establishment of dairy society in the village in 1988, along with other villagers, she too carried milk, both times in almost all seasons to a distance of 1.5 km. Having faced many problems, she mobilised the womenfolk to form an 'all-women' society and with the help of men succeeded in establishing a dairy cooperative society in the village. As expected she was unanimously elected as the chairwoman. All the women requested her to be the secretary and guide the society in all matters.

Chandrikaben's day starts at 5.00 am and she attends work in the cattle shed including cleaning the shed, watering animals, feeding, removing dung, preparation of dung cakes, and milking. She is supported by her sister-in-law (Devarani) in all these works. After taking a cup of tea she attends the work of dairy society as a secretary. She has been getting good support from her brother-in-law, sister-in-law and husband. her husband (Arvind Bhai) studied upto B.A. and is quite understanding and cooperative. Though, she is not having land on her name, she has bought a cow from her parents house (peer) and the income earned from that cow is kept by her only. She has a bank balance of Rs. 5400 and is getting a monthly salary of Rs. 670. She is happy with the performance of the society and is interested in constructing an approach road, a public water-works, and constructing a building for the dairy society with the help of surplus generated and aid from the Amul. She has been encouraging women to purchase more crossbred animals and improve the milk production in the village. To support the milch animals, improved fodder seeds and fodder saplings are distributed through the society and Chandrikaben has been adopting all the new techniques on her farm which is helping as a demonstration unit to the villagers.

When asked about the threat from the Sardar Dairy (a private dairy established in Mehsana), she is confident that all the members will be loyal to the society and not even a single one goes to private traders. She is concerned about the facilities extended by the Amul and help rendered by the supervisor of Amul. She attended (a) Mahila Jagrit Programme, (b) Mahila Seminar, (c) Annual General Body Meetings of the Amul, and (d) a number of committee meetings of the society.

Factors identified for success

1. Young, educated, and enthusiastic personality.
2. Belonging to high caste hindu and landed community.
3. Devotes more time to the occupation and takes necessary care for the development of animals.
4. Close supervision of the enterprise.
5. Support from husband, in-laws and other members of the house.
6. Strong backward and forward linkages extended by the Amul.
7. Managerial abilities.

7.5 Kamalaben Hirabhai Talar (35 Years): Kamalaben was interviewed in field while she was winnowing wheat along with her daughter and husband. She has two daughters and two sons—sons are the youngest. However, she treats all the children equally. Though she is not in a position to support a big family, she desired to have sons as 'they help us in old age and carry our name in the years to come'. She had daughters in the first and second issues. Her elder daughter who studied up to 5th standard married last year and was going to in-laws house on the day of interview. Though, Kamalaben and her husband are illiterate, they encouraged their two daughters to go to school while the sons are too small to go.

They have one acre of dry land, a local cow, a buffalo, and two female calves. Lack of water, green fodder, sufficient capital forced her to keep local animals and poured 1.5 litres of milk to society on the day of visit. She gave 0.5 kg of cattle feed (purchased from the society) and 4 kgs of dry fodder on that day. Thus, the paid out costs are minimum. They also leased in 1.5 acre of land on share cropping basis (she is not aware of the size of land leased in!). They get one-fourth of produce by contributing the labour when required for the agriculture operations. They take tea twice a day, and jowar chapati with vegetables both times. She is a non-vegetarian and cooks meat/chicken on festival occasions. Apart from working on their land, she goes for wage labour where she gets Rs. 12–18 per day and one time meal, two tea and some snuff. Though she is a founder member and pouring milk to the society, she takes little interest in the society's activities. She is of the opinion that developmental programmes are meant for rich, literate, high caste hindu, and landed community only. Certain amount of pessimistic thinking is also noticed in her.

Reasons for failure

1. Lack of sound financial base,
2. Illiteracy,
3. Low caste hindu,
4. Unaware of developmental programmes, and
5. Unfavourable market conditions.

7.6 Anandben Ashokbhai Patel: Anandben studied upto 9th standard and hails from one of the progressive villages of Cambay Taluka. Her parents too studied up to 10th standard and her lonely sister passed the teacher training course. She has two sons, a daughter and has undergone tubectomy operation in a private hospital. She is living in a nuclear family and her husband studied upto 7th standard. They have 2 acres of irrigated land, all on her husband's name only, and a crossbred cow and two improved buffaloes of which she owned one. She is fortunate enough to have such a nice husband and she takes the major decisions like variety to sow, size of animals to be kept, purchase of clothes to children, purchasing durable assets, child bearing, etc. She attributes her husband's attitude to her membership in the village milk society. She still remembers the problems faced by her when she took milk to Khatnal (prior to 1986) which included: (a) long distance, (b) recording low fat percentages, (c) irregular payment, (d) evading payment, (e) high cost of feed, (f) problem in taking animals to AI centre and dispensary, etc. However, all the problems are the history of the past. She is very much interested with the services rendered by the society. Though, it is a mixed gender society, the committee members gave considerable importance to issues related to women. These included: providing protected water tanks in the village, encouraging social foresty to mitigate fuel scarcity, construction of approach road, school, etc.

On an average, she earns Rs. 400–450 per month, after meeting all expenses in maintaining animals. Last year they purchased 0.50 acre of land out of the savings generated from the agriculture and milk business. She is also planning to purchase two more crossbreds so that she can earn more money out of the work. Apart from attending household chores, she practically attends to all operations pertaining to animals. Her husband does not know milking and cannot help her in this work. Anandben wants to educate her sons, get them employed in a bank and college. She likes her sons to daughter as they help in taking her to heaven. Hence, she feels that it is not appropriate to assign any work—particularly work related to animals to sons. However, her daughter attends to almost all works pertaining to animals and household.

7.7 Santaben Dudabhai: Forty-eight-year old Santaben is a widow who came back to her natal village after the untimely death of her husband who was working in a school. She has no issues. Seven years ago she managed to dispose of her husband's land and purchased 3.5 acres in her natal village. As it is a dry village, she makes her living from dairying. She has two local buffaloes and is living in her elder brother's house which is a thatched house with cow dung flooring. She availed loan from Bank of Baroda to purchase a buffalo and the loan amount was repaid in time. During the year 1993-94, she sold 1050 litres of milk to the society which fetched an amount of Rs. 8162. Further, she also sold 150 litres to neighbourers at the rate of Rs. 8.10 per litre. Thus, she earned an income of Rs. 9377 after consuming 150 litres of milk in that year. While dry fodder, and seasonal green fodder is available from her land, labour is unpaid, she spent Rs. 5.25 per day on concentrates and Rs. 211 on veterinary expenses. Though, she is happy with the quality and price of the Amul dan, she is unhappy about the quality of veterinary services. As a matter of fact, route veterinary doctor visits the village once in 15 days and she wants this visit once in a week.

Santaben is very much satisfied by the other services rendered by the society. She being illiterate, gets information on clean milk production, etc. from her brother who studied up to 10th standard. She is interested in attending the training programmes and proposes to visit Amul dairy. She is proud to be a member of the society, and is of the opinion that society helped to provide income and employment and increased her status in the village.

7.8 Santaben Purushottambhai (35 years) : Illiterate Santaben has four daughters and a son. Her husband, who studied up to 5th tried to convince her to undergo tubectomy after second daughter. As Santaben was very much interested in having a son, they had two more daughters and finally a son. She is happy because she feels that 'my son will look after me when I am old, he will carry my name and help us sending to heaven'. They have one local buffalo and female calf purchased with the help of a bank loan. Two of her elder daughters are going to school and rest are yet to start. Last year they supplied Rs. 1050 worth of milk to the society. Their yields are low because of non-availability of green fodder and concentrates. She admits that she gets the fodder from 'other fields' either in the early hours or late nights. She also takes the animal for grazing. She tends 12 animals belonging to others at the rate of Rs. 10 per month and gets a monthly income of Rs. 120. While cattle tending is restricted to only afternoon hours, she also works as labour both morning and evening at the rate of Rs. 8 per shift of 3.5 hours. June, September, December, and February are the peak agricultural months and she gets a daily wage of Rs. 16 and two tea but no food. In all, she gets wage for 100–120 days a year. She is the first to get up from the bed and also last to go to bed in the house. Her husband also works with her and is habituated to smoking and occasionally drinks country made liquor. She has not complained about harassment but they quarrel when he drinks. She also has 4 hens and a cock which will be used on special occasion/festival. She wants to educate all her daughters and get them married in the nearby villages. Santaben has complained about the (a) nonavailability of fuel wood in the village which is taking 1–2 hours of her daily time, (b) need for public lavotaries for women, (c) a high school for children, and (d) sufficient drinking water for people and cattle. She once visited Amul dairy and was happy with the services provided by the milk union.

Santaben's daily routine is as under

Activity	Duration
a) Getting up from bed	5.00AM
b) Cleaning animals and shed, feeding, milking	5.15–6.30 AM
c) Preparation of tea	6.35–6.45 AM
d) Bringing water	6.45–7.15 AM
e) Cleaning clothes	7.15–7.45 AM
f) Going to field work	8.00–12.00 noon
g) Preparation of food	12.00–1.00 PM
h) Collection of wood and fodder	1.00–2.00 PM
i) Lunch and rest	2.00–3.00 PM
j) Field work	3.00–6.00 PM
k) Bringing water	3.00–3.30 PM
l) Cleaning animals, shed, and feeding, watering animals	3.30–5.00 PM
m) Milking and carrying milk to society	5.30–6.00 PM
n) Cleaning house and utensils	6.00–7.00 PM
o) Preparation of food	7.00–8.00 PM
p) Cleaning utensils and talking to children	8.00–9.00PM
q) Going to bed	9.00 PM

7.9 Champaben Ramanbhai (29 years): Champaben hails from Parmar (Kshatriya) community and was married to a landless at the age of 19. Her father was a school teacher and she being the youngest in the house got all freedom to study in the childhood. She was treated well by her parents, her parents liked her more compared to her brothers. They have two sons, one is in second standard and the other in first standard. When self employed women's association (SEWA) introduced its health care programme, village women unanimously elected Champaben as health worker. She has undergone 6 months training in child care, pre and post natal health care, and human nutrition. She is getting a salary of Rs. 500 per month. Her job includes weighing of newly born children, health checkups, pregnant women checkups, and attending to common ailments. In case of serious cases, she admits the women/children in the hospital located at Anand, which is 8 km away from the village. All the intending patients are to pay Rs. five as membership fee and details pertaining to them are recorded on card specially prepared for each member.

As she is working, her husband takes care of almost all the household works including milking, cattle keeping, etc.

He also works as a farm labourer. She has two local buffaloes which gave 2004 litres of milk during 1993–94 of which 1304 litres sold to the milk society, 200 litres to the neighbourers, and the rest 500 litres was used for home consumption. Their total family income for the same period is Rs. 12506 of which income from dairying constituted 32%, 20% from agricultural labour and thus, leaving as much as 48% from service. She has a bank balance of Rs. 13,000 in Bank of Baroda. As she is the principle earner, she takes major decisions in the household including purchase of clothes, utensils, children's education, etc. She caste her vote in the recently held assembly elections and interestingly she advised her husband to vote to a particular party. Since, she is not taking care of animals, she has little knowledge of the functioning of the society. Nevertheless, she is happy about the services provided by it. She is against the entry of private dairies and decided to sell milk to cooperative society only. Though she is not aware of Beijing women's conference, she opines that women in the highest levels of government are an exception throughout the world. She wanted both her children to become doctors, so that they can help the villagers. She had undergone a number of training programmes, visited Amul, and attended co-operative development programme meant for women members.

In her opinion, both son and daughter are equal, there shouldn't be any discrimination. She had family planning operation after two sons as it would have been difficult to look after a big family. On an average she spends one-and-half to two hours a day with children, helping them in completing home work, reading their books, and some times visit their school to monitor their progress. They also go for a picnic/pilgrimage once in a month. Champaben opines that 'intelligence is not gender specific'. Women should be involved in the planning and decision making process and thus can bring a sense of belongingness among them. She is of the opinion that 'all women' dairy cooperatives can be used as a means to achieve this objective.

7.10 Bikhiben Patel (35 years): Bikhiben has two sons studying B. Com and 7th standard. Her husband is having 6.5 acres of land, a tractor and scooter. He finds little time to help

Bikhiben and mostly engrossed in farm work only. He treats Bikhiben very well, they go outing once in a month. Though she studied up to 7th standard, she has been elected as a Chairwoman during this year because of her straight forwardness, and social works. Bikhiben is of the opinion that the committee meetings should be held in the premises of the society and not in somebody's house. She strictly follows circulating the agenda book to all the committee members and makes sure that all members are informed about the monthly meetings.

Bikhiben has five crossbred cows, one buffalo and 3 female calves of which the buffalo was given by parents at the time of her marriage. They sold another buffalo which too she got from her parents and the sale proceeds were given to her husband. She has a bank account and kept her 'Streedhan' in it. These animals gave 6050 litres of milk sold worth of Rs. 39,400 during 1993–94. As they have 6 animals she hardly finds time to go to field work and mostly busy with feeding, watering, cleaning, and milking these animals. She personally carrys milk to the society daily and also helps the society employees in managing the accounts, etc. When asked about preference towards children, Bikhiben is of the opinion that both male and female child is equal. However, she opted for tubectomy after the birth of her second son. As of work related to cattle, and house, she is of the firm opinion that it is the female's work and men should not attend this work. She prefers to assign such work to a paid labour than asking her sons/husband to help her in such activities. She believes that there is no perfect substitute to breast milk and fed milk to her two sons till 20 months of their age. She is also aware that the fore milk is thin and contains less fat while hind milk is thicker and full of fats which is true in both human and animal milk.

As to know the working of a milk society, she visited 3 men managed societies nearby and also Amul. She is very confident that given the training, and education, women can manage business enterprises efficiently than men. It is so because: women are more sincere, there will be no unnecessary expenditure, less scope for mismanagement, less scope for quarrelling, they are more dedicated and hard working.

Her future plans are (a) constructing a building for the milk society, (b) construction of an approach road of 1.5 km to the village, and (c) bringing protected water scheme to the village by digging a bore well in the village.

7.11 Lalitaben Bikhabhai (28 years): Household woman turned milk tester, Lalitaben belongs to Patel community and having 7 acres of land on her husband's name. She has two crossbred cows of her own. She studied up to seventh standard and has a daughter and son, both are going to school in the same village. When she got married, there was no milk society in the village and she too carried milk for a distance of 1.5 km. When the idea of forming an 'all-women' dairy society was mooted villagers selected her unanimously as milk tester and 4 day training was given at the society in conducting fat and SNF tests. Now, she is confident of testing on milkotester and taking lactometre reading. The total gross income of the household for the year 1993–94 was Rs. 76688 of which income from dairying accounted for 49% followed by income from agriculture (42%), and the rest from her service. Initially, she was not interested in the job thinking that joining society and sitting before village elders, etc. was not good. However, villagers persuaded her which she accepted and with the help of women, she has been able to overcome all the difficulties.

Lalitaben is of the opinion that the presence of society has increased her work-load. She is to attend the household chores, to look after all activities connected with cattle keeping, and society work. Her husband doesn't know milking even today. There is absolutely no help from the husband in the above works. She feels the burden of increased work. However it was overlooked by the enhanced income from dairying. She is the real owner of the money. Prior to becoming member, and working in the society, she used to ask her husband for money several times. But, now it is reversed. He has to ask and give account for each and every penny. They all go for a picture twice in a year and she takes major decisions in the house. She got tubectomised against wishes of her husband. She voted for the party she liked while husband voted for another party in the recent elections. When asked about automatic machines (weighing, testing, and accounting) she conveyed her ignorance but was confident of handling it with the support and training given by the officials of Amul. She is interested in purchasing another crossbred cow, sending her children to college in Anand, having an approach road to the village, and drinking water facility in the village. She says that 'I am a housewife and love cooking, not only the gujarati foods but also south Indian dishes like idli, dosa, vada, etc. and argues that women should be given opportunities in village panchayats also.

7.12 Rewaben Eshwarbhai (30 years): Rewaben hails from Kshatriya community and popularly known as Chief Minister in the locality, because of her sportive, talkative nature and dashing qualities. Her native place is 40 km away and got married at the age of 15. She has a daughter who is 4 years old and is eagerly looking for a son. Her father-in-law is staying with them. They have limited assets, and planning to have a fan. The house is of 200 sq feet with only one living room and small verandha. Though, she is illiterate she is good at managing her house, and farm. She is the decision maker in the house. She has two sisters and two brothers, one of the sisters got married in the same village. They have good relations too. Her day starts at 6.00 AM. She gets 2 hours rest in the afternoon and spends 2–3 hours in collecting fuel wood. She has to wander 2–3 km for getting fuel wood, and sometimes owners harass, scold, quarrel, etc. They have two cots, 3 big storage bins and some utensils to cook. Her husband is not alcoholic and believes in god but smokes beedi. Quarrels are not frequent in the house. She works for 175 days as agricultural labour in a year and husband works for 125–135 days. Mostly husband obliges her and if he does not, 'he won't get food that day'. They go to picture once in a year at Anand. They visited Ahmedabad, Dakor, Ambaji, Mount Abu, etc. They have 0.50 acre of irrigated land on which they take bajra and tobacco. The family is also supported by two murrah buffaloes and two female calves. In addition to owned land, they took 1.5 acres on share cropping basis. While the land is given by the owner, they provide all the labour required. Further, expenditure and output is shared equally between the owner and share cropper. Bajra, tobacco, and green fodder are grown on this land while the water is purchased from the neighbourer's tubewell. They have been doing this for the last 4 years. Total gross income of the family was Rs. 14582 of which 55.4% came from sale of milk, 20.6% from agriculture and the rest from agricultural labour. All the work related to animals are taken care of by her only and husband does not know even milking. In case she visits her parents' village, her sister helps in milking their buffalo. They took Rs. 8000 from the State Bank of India to purchase two buffaloes of which Rs. 2500 is outstanding. Once it is repaid, she intends to purchase one more buffalo with help of bank loan. She visited Amul once and was very much impressed about the functioning of the union. They had kichidi, brinjal curry, and milk in the dinner (last night) while bajra roti, potato curry and green chillies comprised their lunch. When asked about the educated and working couples, she maintains that 'working couples are not faithful to each other'. According to Rewaben, common toilets are the need of the hour. All the women have been facing lot of difficulty in the absence of common toilets. Similarly, she intends to promote social forestry on the village common land such that demand for fuel wood can be met. She believes in cooperation and opines that all milk producers should come together to support Amul. Income and expenditure statement provided by Rewaben is quite interesting.

Cost and return from milch buffalo (per annum is given in the table on page 96).

However, it is to be mentioned here that the cost of labour and fodder (both green and dry) are not out of pocket expenses which works out to Rs. 9575 leaving only Rs. 2680 as paid out costs.

7.13 Summary

A study of the individual case studies revealed that a vast majority of the women benefited out of the dairy business. Dairying helped in increasing employment and income. The increased incomes are utilized for a variety of purposes of their choice. As a result of economic independence, their sta-

Cost and return from milch buffalo (per annum)

Particulars	Amount (Rs.)
Milk yield	
4 litres × 250 days	
(Rs./litre 8.00)	8000
Income from dung	250
Calf value (female)	1500
Gross income	9750
Insurance	320
Interest on fixed investment	960
Family labour (@ Rs. 10×365)	3650
Medicines	150
Green fodder (10 kgs @ 25 paise/kg for 180 days if purchases)	450
Dry fodder (10 bundles per day @ Rs. 1.50 per bundle for 365 days	5475
Amul concentrate (2 kg per day @ 2.50 for 250 days)	1250
Gross cost	12255
Net profit/loss	–2505

tus in the house and in the society has substantially improved. It also boosted their self-confidence, and participation in decision making process. Dairying also exposed them to a number of developmental activities and thus helped in widening their horizon and thought process. However, benefits realised are more in landed, high caste hindu families than 'others'. Lack of resources, illiteracy, lack of knowledge, etc. are responsible for such low realisations on small and landless households. Though there is an increase in the workload, as a result of expansion of animal holdings, the benefits accrued out weighed the burden/pains. Majority of women respondents wanted to expand size of the animal holding provided credit is made available through financial institutions. On the whole, men folk cooperated and extended necessary support for successful operation of the activity.

8

Summary and Conclusions

8.1 Introduction

Animal husbandry has been an integral part of the Indian agriculture. There is a symbiotic relationship between crop and animal agriculture. Apart from providing milk, these animals performed multiple roles such as providing power, dung, conservation, animal byproducts, recreation, etc. However, due to change in our priorities, current emphasis is on crossbreeding. While the men looked after agricultural operations, women took care of animal husbandry. Women are familiar with all activities involved in raising animals and they are associated with it from their childhood. However, their role in animal husbandry is less recognized and are treated as invisible workers. Efforts have been made by a few organisations to recognise their role and bring them under cooperative fold and Amul is one such organisation.

8.2 Objectives of the Study

Present study is an attempt to evaluate the performance of women managed dairy cooperatives vis-a-vis men managed dairy cooperatives and draw lessons for future policy planning exercises. Specific objectives of the study are:

(a) to observe the progress of Amul during 1947–95,
(b) to study the socio-economic profile of selected villages, and farmers,

(c) to analyse the structure and performance of women and men managed dairy cooperative societies, and identify the factors responsible for success and/or failure of women managed societies,
(d) to understand the status of women during pre and post enrolment in the dairy society,
(e) to work out training needs of women cooperators for successful operation of the society, and
(f) to document profiles of selected women dairy farmers.

8.3 Summary of the Results

Summary of the results are presented in six sections: (a) profile of the district and Amul, (b) socio-economics of selected villages, (c) structure and performance of dairy societies, (d) status of women during pre and post enrolment, (e) effectiveness of cooperative education, and (f) women dairy farmers profiles.

8.3.1 Profile of the district and Amul

Kaira district has the advantage of good soil, improved buffaloes, crossbred cows, hard working, sincere and innovative farmers, entrepreneurs like Pestonji Polson, committed leaders like Sardar Vallabh Bhai Patel, Shri Morarji Desai, and Shri Tribhuvandas Patel, and technocrats like Dr. V. Kurien and Shri H.M. Dalaya and their colleagues. Thus, Amul was evolved out of the felt needs of producers, supported by local leaders and having large urban market (Bombay) for the milk produced in rural areas. Though there were some government protections in the initial periods, combined efforts of producers, leaders and technocrats lead the union to come out as one of the few successful examples in India. A number of countries have shown interest in replicating this model.

There has been a spectacular growth in almost all the performance parameters studied during the period 1947–95. Interestingly, the management of Amul has realised the role of women in milk production, management of animals, and did considerable work to bring them under the fold of dairy cooperatives. As a result, the percentage of women in the total membership has increased from 7.6% during 1960–61 to about 15% during 1994–95. There are 10 'all women' dairy cooperative societies in the union.

8.3.2 Socio-economics of selected villages

Selected villages represented three different ecologies of Kaira district. Of the 6 societies, three were established prior to 1970 and rest in the later half of 1980s. In terms of quality of soil, availability of ground water, productivity of animals, general economic conditions, etc., Khadgodhra is in a disadvantageous position. There is a positive correlation between population/agricultural land and bovine population but a negative correlation exists between size of the stock and productivity. As a result, cost of milk procurement per litre of milk collected is the lowest, Rs. 0.29, in Ghadiana Timba while it is the highest, Rs. 0.49, in Khadgodhra. Average age of women members is relatively less than men members. The distribution of land holdings is more skewed than the distribution of animal holdings. Similarly, only 8% of women members have land on their name while as many as 36% of them have their own animals. About 82% and 73% of milk produced is sold to the milk societies in both women and men managed societies respectively; sales to 'others' are negligible. Women utilized their savings on purchase of consumer durables, milch animals, gold, etc., while men gave priority to consumer durables, ceremonies and milch animals in that order.

8.3.3 Structure and performance of dairy societies

These dairy societies are managed by a nine member management committee and the day to day operations are looked after by paid staff comprising a secretary, milk collector, tester, etc. Physical and financial performance indicators studied included membership, milk collection, average per member contribution, sour milk, net profit, cost of procurement, etc. When measured on the above parameters, women managed societies fared relatively better during the study period (1990–94). Men managed societies realised better price as they maintained mostly buffaloes. Rate of conception (%) is better in women managed societies and hence they are happy with the quality of AI services provided by the union. Similarly, women managed societies did well in providing milk production enhancement inputs too. As of management committee, involvement of women members in terms of number of meetings conducted, average attendance, frequency of interaction with officials of Amul, etc. is again on the higher side. Both categories of societies contributed to the village amenities. There is a shift of power from village panchayats to milk societies. Average monthly salary/employee is less in women managed societies but the average milk procurement/employee is more. The study has shown that given equal access to resources and human capital, women can perform significantly better than men. As regards quality of services provided, there are not many significant differences in the opinion of members. On the basis of above findings, factors responsible for the success of the women managed societies are identified.

8.3.4 Status of women

Data on female labour participation in household, agriculture, and animal husbandry revealed that women worked for, on an average, 16 hours/day during the post enrolment period, their work increased by 3.5 hours/day during this period. No male-female wage differentials are observed in the study area. Across various sectors, their participation declined in agriculture while that in household, and dairying increased. Participation of women in decision making in agriculture and dairying indicated that there is significant improvement in decision making, more so in dairying, during the post enrolment period. Respondents from landed household, high caste hindu families with higher education exerted more power than others. As of status of women, 76% of the sample respondents have indicated that it has increased, while only 5% opined that it has decreased.

8.3.5 Effectiveness of cooperative education

The study of the effectiveness of training programmes indicated that majority of respondents are interested in undergoing training programmes and also they are aware of the effectiveness and utility of the programmes. About 71% of the respondents interviewed are trained during the last 5 years and their ability with regard to breeding, feeding, health care, and general management has fairly increased as a result of training programme. As regards future training requirements respondents of landless and small holdings indicated family planning, child care, and clean milk production as their priorities, while leadership development, and crop cultivation by medium and large holdings. Majority of the respondents have shown their willingness to attend training programme of about 3 days duration outside the village and would like to have training from women trainers.

8.3.6 Women dairy farmers' profiles

A study of the individual case studies revealed that a vast majority of the women benefited from the dairy business. Dairying helped in increasing employment and income. The increased incomes are utilized for a variety of purposes of their choice. As a result of economic independence, their status in the house and in the society has substantially improved. Dairying also exposed them to a number of developmental activities and thus helped in widening their horizon and thought process. It also boosted their self confidence, and participation in decision making process. However, benefits realised are more in landed, high caste hindu families than 'others', probably because of land, resources, and access to media. Lack of resources, illiteracy, lack of knowledge, etc. are responsible for such low realisations in the lower income groups. Though there is an increase in the workload, as a result of expansion of animal holdings and associated work, the benefits accrued out-weighed the burden/pains. Majority of the women respondents interviewed wanted to expand size of the animal holding provided credit was made available through financial institutions. On the whole, men folk cooperated and extended necessary support for successful operation of the activity. The credit goes to CD programme which motivated male members to encourage/support women which took a lot of time and effort of the group members.

8.4 Conclusions

The study revealed that women are equally capable and in some cases performed better than men in managing democratic organisations like milk societies. These organisations succeeded, to a great extent, in providing both social and economic empowerment to women. In order to support women in general and 'all-women' dairy cooperative societies in particular, the following suggestions are made for policy.

Apart from inducting women into cooperatives, necessary training in scientific milk production, leadership building, sanitation, philosophy of cooperation, and general management should be imparted. The strategy of the 'all-women' dairy cooperative societies should be (a) to awaken creative potential of women for their welfare and for the welfare of the nation, (b) to generate employment and income opportunities for the farm women in rural areas, and (c) to improve leadership qualities based on democratic principles. As most of the women do not have rights on land, government should provide loans without any collateral obligations. They should also be informed about the loaning procedures. Young and educated women should be given the opportunity to work in the primary milk societies as secretaries, testers, etc. As to reduce gender gaps in literacy and increase participation in decision making, government with help of voluntary organisations, should arrange adult education programmes and also should convince parents to send girl children to schools. Literacy training for women and increased education for girls will increase productivity and empowerment both today and in future. The focus should be on the girl child and it should be linked with the development of women. It is expected that through improvement in socio-economic status, women get a key role in decision making in the family and in the society, thus paving the way for the gradual obliteration of their vulnerability. Training should be imparted through women trainers. So as to represent the interests of women, 1/3rd of the committee members in mixed gender societies should be earmarked to women. If women are to be persons in their own right, they must be in control of their own bodies and suitably empowered.

Village women should organise Mahila Mandals whose aim has been organisation of women and creating awareness among them to work for betterment of family and society by fully involving in the process of development. The end result will be the socio-economic transformation of the villages. They have to be entrusted with the responsibility of disseminating scientific findings and monitoring their reception/rejection. Mahila Mandals should take the responsibility of changing age old cultural factors and some of the ideological prejudices which inhibit the development of women.

Women in the study area are fortunate to the extent that legislation has given them a right to equal inheritance in the non-coparcenary families. Women should effectively utilize this right and also claim a right over the coparcenary property in order to seek a de-facto rather than de-jure readjustment of the social institutions to their own advantage which will enhance their economic empowerment. The recent 73rd and 74th amendments to our constitution go a long way in providing political empowerment to women.

The number of milk societies and the membership has now reached saturation and for increased production the union should focus its attention on (a) mobilising women members, and (b) increasing the stock of improved animals. An integrated approach for improving the productivity of both pastures and animals is needed. Since majority of the villages are rainfed, necessary arrangements should be made to exploit ground water potential which will increase both crop yields as well as availability of green and dry fodder. Simultaneously, efforts should also be made to increase the area under fodder crops. In this context union should initiate action to bring village common lands, waste lands, vacant land alongside railway track, etc. to cultivate both energy and protein rich fodder crops. Necessary inputs required for the same may also be made available on cost to cost basis to the producers through primary societies. Improvement in the productivity of pastures through soil conservation measures and reseeding them with nutritive forages would reduce labour in tending cattle. Efforts will have to be intensified to upgrade buffaloes, and crossbreeding in cattle with superior germ plasm. Network of health care facilities should be strengthened to the best satisfaction of the producer members. This will go a long way in strengthening the relationship between union and producer members. The union should arrange a dialogue between veterinarians, animal nutritionists, officials of the union, social scientists, and women. Such dialogues will result in finding out mechanisms for regular flow of information and feedback.

Union should also concentrate on production of value added commodities and plough back part of its profits to the primaries so as to sustain member loyalty. Further, the union should maintain constant touch with the members so as to know their requirements/feelings lest private dairies make use of the situation to their advantage. In this context, it is suggested to strengthen the field extension activities. The Union should also keep an eye on the societies' accounts so as to eliminate unscrupulous elements in the organisation of primaries.

In order to reduce percentage of sour milk, and to make procurement producer friendly, more and more village chilling units should be established wherever there is enough milk procurement. Similarly, electronic milk collection units may also be installed in such big villages. Installation of electronic milk units go a long way in keeping upto date records of transactions, drastically reduces the work of paid staff, and is error free. This will also enable reducing expenditure on stationery. The system of awarding medals/merit certificates to the best performing societies procuring large quantities of good quality milk may be continued.

References

Boserup, E. (1970), Women's role in economic development, St. Martin's Press, New York.

Charlton, S.E.M. (1984), Women in third world development, Westview Press, London.

Dak, T.M., M.L. Sharma, and R. Jain (1986), Social and institutional framework of female participation in agriculture, Indian Journal of Social Work, 48(3): 285–291.

Datta, S., S. Das, and J. Basu (1995), Effect of gender role identity on gender role attitude in women, Journal of Community Guidance and Research, 12(1): 55–62.

Department of Social Welfare (1975), Towards equality, Report of the committee on the status of women in India, Government of India, New Delhi.

Director of Census Population (1992), Census of India, 1991, Gujarat series 7, Supplement of paper I of 1991, Government of Gujarat, Ahmedabad.

Directorate of Animal Husbandry (1990), Bulletin of animal husbandry and dairying status 1988–89, Government of Gujarat, Ahmedabad.

Directorate of Economics and Statistics (1991), Quarterly bulletin of Economics and statistics, Government of Gujarat, Gandhinagar 31(1): 1–3.

Directorate of Economics and Statistics (1992), Socio-economic survey of Gujarat state 1992–93, Government of Gujarat, Gandhinagar.

Economic and Social Commission for Asia and the Pacific (1981), Participation of women in dairy development in South Asia, Report of a workshop, United Nations, Bangkok.

Gadgil, D.R. (1938), The industrial evolution in India in recent times, Oxford University Press, Bombay.

Goetz, A.M. (1991), Feminism and the claim to know: Contradictions in faminist approaches women in development, in Grant, R. and K. Neeuland (eds.), Gender and international relations, Open University Press, Milton Keynes, pp. 133–157.

Khandwalla, P.N. (1987), Organisational behaviour for social development: A position paper, Paper presented at the international conference on organisational and behavioural perspectives for social development, held at IIM, Ahmedabad during December 29, 1986 to January 2, 1987.

Leacock, E. (1986), Women power and authority, in Dube, L., E. Leacock, and S. Ardener (eds.), Visibility and power, Oxford University Press, Delhi.

Mies, M., K. Lalita, and K. Kumari (1986), Indian women in subsistence and agricultural labour, Women, work and development 12, International Labour Office, Geneva.

Mitra, M. (1984). Women in dairying in Andhra Pradesh (mimeo), The Hague Institute of Social Studies, The Hague.

Mitra, M. (1987), Women's work: Gains analysis of women's labour in dairy production, in Singh, A.M. and A. Kelles-Viitanen (eds.), Invisible hands: Women in homebased production, Sage Publications, New Delhi.

Mitra M. (1990), Profiles of women dairy producers in Andhra Pradesh, in Doornbos, M. and K.N. Nair (eds.), Resources, institutions strategies: Operation flood and Indian dairying, Sage Publications, New Delhi.

Nagabrahmam D. (1987), Cooperative dairying in India, Kurukshetra, 35(11): 4–6.

National commission on self employed women and women in the informal sector (1988), Shramshakti, NCSEWWIS, New Delhi.

NDDB (undated), The present status of women in India, Cooperative development group, NDDB, Anand.

NDDB (1987), Model byelaws: Primary milk producers' cooperative society, NDDB, Anand.

NDDB (1989), Cooperative development programme of the NDDB, NDDB, Anand.

NDDB (1993), National women's dairy programme, NDDB, Anand.

NDDB (1994a), Women's dairy cooperative development: Volume-III, NDDB, Anand.

NDDB (1994b), Women's dairy cooperative leadership programme, NDDB, Anand.

NDDB (1994c), Impact study of cooperative development programme: Bulandshahar milk union, NDDB, Anand.

Patel, C.I. (1995), Assessment for actualising the targetted potential of increase in procurement of milk in Amul, HDCM Project report, Udaybhansinhji Institute of Cooperative Management, Gandhinagar.

Patel, S. (1990), The Anand Pattern: A socio-historical analysis of its origin and growth, in Doornbs, M. and K.N. Nair (eds.) (1990), Resources, institutions and strategies: Operation flood and Indian dairying, Indo-Dutch studies on development alternatives-4, Sage Publications, New Delhi.

Planning Commission (1981), Sixth five year plan: 1980–85, Government of India, New Delhi.

Planning Commission (1993), Annual plan: 1992–93, Government of India, New Delhi.

Rao, V.M. (1985), Can women manage enterprises: A case of Piparia cooperative milk society (Amul) (mimeo), VMNICM, Pune.

Reddy, K.P. and S. Sharma (1990), Decision styles of chief executives and organisational performance in dairy cooperative unions, Workshop Report No. 4, IRMA, Anand.

Revenue Department (1983), Report on agricultural census: Gujarat state 1980–81, Government of Gujarat, Gandhinagar.

Ruben, G. (1975), The traffic in women: Notes on the political economy of sex, in Reiter (ed.), Towards an anthropology of women (original not seen), quoted in Chakravarti, U., and K. Roy (1988), In search of your past: A review of the limitations and possibilities of the histography of women in early India, Economic and Political Weekly, 23(18): WS2-WS10.

Saradamoni, K. (1987), Labour, land and rice production: Women's involvement in three states, Economic and Political Weekly, 27(17): WS2-WS6.

Sen, D., and J. Rani (1990), Women in dairying: A case study, Journal of Rural Development, 9(5): 809–831.

Sethi, R.M. (1991), Women in agriculture, Rawat Publications, New Delhi.

Shah, T. (1990), Reppo:teur's report on learning from success: Analytical review of successful farmers and farmers' cooperatives, Indian Journal of Agricultural Economics, 45(3): 419–431.

Shah, T. (1991), Management of a village dairy cooperative society: Field notes from Laxmipura (Sabarkantha), IRMA, Anand.

Sharma, M., and U. Vanjani (1989), Women's work is never done: Dairy 'development' and health in the lives of rural women in Rajasthan, Economic and Political Weekly, 24(17): WS 38-WS 44.

Sobha, V. (1987), Rural women and development: A study of female agricultural labourers in Telangana, Mittal Publications, Delhi.

Somjee, A.H. and G. Somjee (1978), Cooperative dairying and the profiles of social change in India, Economic Development and Cultural Change, 26(3): 577–590.

Somjee, G., and A.H. Somjee (1989), Reaching out to the poor: The unfinished rural revolution, Macmillan, London.

Steers, R.M. (1975), Problems in the measurement of organisational effectiveness, Administrative Science Quarterly, 20: 546–558.

Spodek, H. (1994), Review article: The self-employed women's association (SEWA) in India: Feminist, Gandhian power in development, Economic Development and Cultural Change, 43(1): 193–202.

Sundar, P. (1981), Khadgodhra: A case study of women's cooperative, Social Action, 31(1): 79–98.

Tantray, A.M. (1991), Participation of women in farm activities, Indian Journal of Extension Education, 27(3 and 4): 134–137.

Thakur, D.S. (1974), Impact of dairy development through milk cooperatives: A case study of Gujarat, Indian Journal of Agricultural Economics, 30(3): 83–89.

Tripathi, H. and H.P.S. Arya (1994), Decision making pattern of farm women in animal husbandry enterprise, Decision, 21(3): 171–178.

Walpole, R.E. (1968), Introduction to statistics, The Macmillan Company, New York, pp. 236–241.

Whyte, R.O. (1982), The women of rural Asia: Westview special studies on women in contemporary societies, Westview Press, Boulder, Colorodo.

Zhang, Y. (1995), A high priced slot in the world of work, World of Work, 12 (May/June): 4–10.

APPENDIX B

Profile of cooperative milk unions affiliated to Gujarat State Cooperative Milk Marketing Foundation (GCMMF), Anand (1993–94)

Union	Number of milk societies	No. of 'all women' societies	Total membership (in '000)	Women members (in '000)	% of women to total membership	Annual milk procurement (lakh tonnes)	Average annual per member milk collection (litres)
Ahmedabad	577 (6.46)	24	52 (3.09)	7 (2.40)	13.46	0.31 (2.85)	602.1
Banaskantha	1082 (12.2)	06	91 (5.41)	7 (2.40)	7.69	0.86 (7.90)	937.3
Baroda	918 (10.29)	17	156 (9.28)	30 (10.27)	19.23	0:57 (5.23)	364.3
Bharuch	490 (5.49)	06	38 (2.26)	3 (1.03)	7.89	0.09 (0.83)	242.9
Gandhinagar	NA	05	12 (0.71)	2 (0.68)	16.67	NA	NA
Kaira	943 (10.56)	10	513 (30.52)	75 (25.69)	14.62	2.70 (24.79)	526.6
Mehsana	1009 (11.31)	02	290 (17.25)	95 (32.54)	32.76	2.91 (26.72)	1004.8
Panchmahal	932 (10.44)	15	108 (6.43)	22 (7.53)	20.37	0.43 (3.95)	393.1
Rajkot	388 (4.35)	NA	30 (1.79)	1 (0.34)	3.33	0.12 (1.10)	421.9
Sabarkantha	1297 (14.53)	06	182 (10.83)	12 (4.11)	6.59	1.50 (13.78)	826.3
Surat	849 (9.51)	32	158 (9.40)	27 (9.25)	17.09	1.09 (10.00)	689.8
Valsad	441 (4.94)	171	51 (3.03)	11 (3.76)	21.57	0.31 (2.85)	598.3
Total	8926 (100.00)	294	1681 (100.00)	292 (100.00)	17.37	10.89 (100.00)	652.5

Source : Office of the GCMMF

APPENDIX A

Organisational chart of Amul

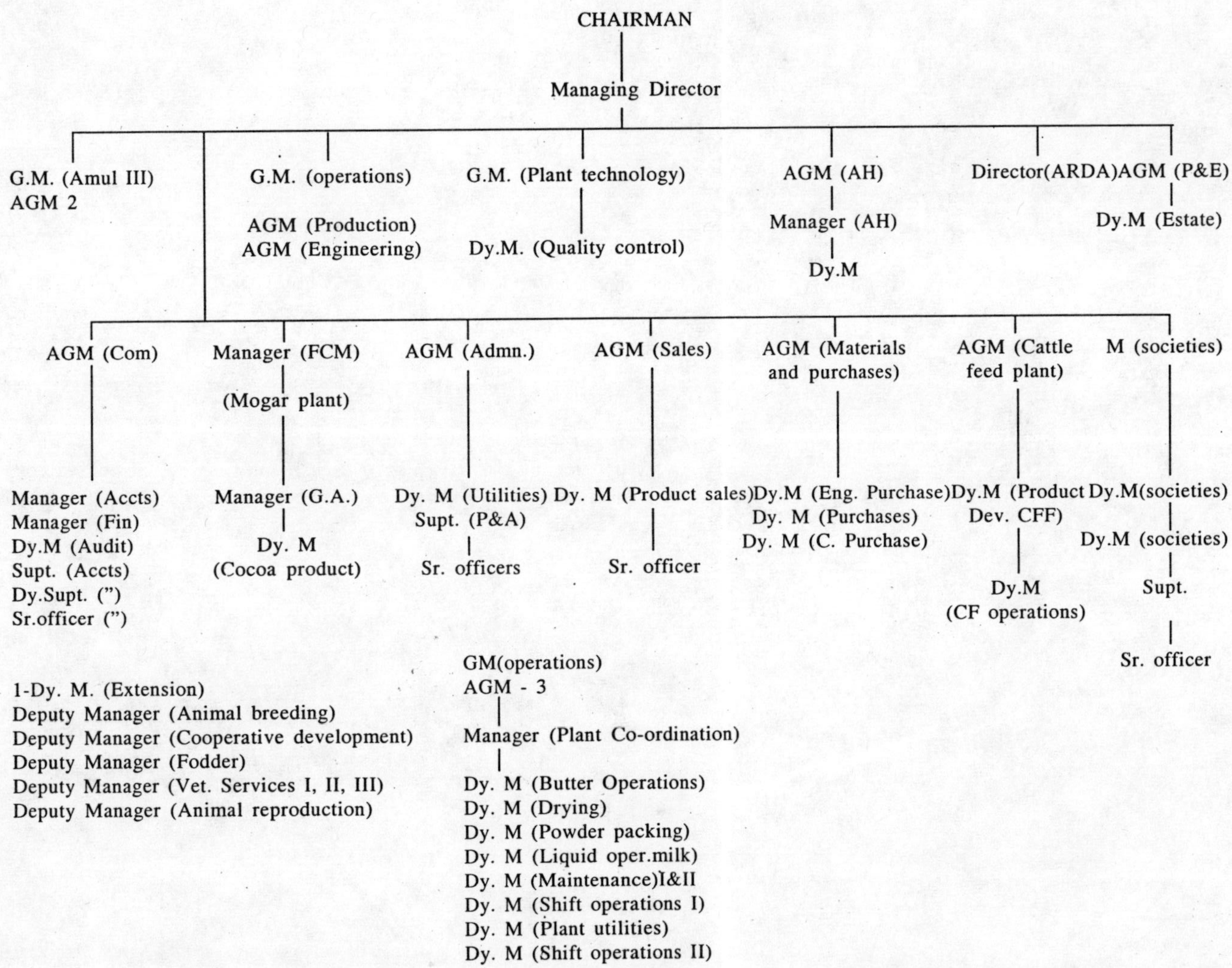

In all there are 55 senior officers upto the category of deputy manager.
There are about 2300 employees working in the union of which 12 are women.